The Dance

Our Journey Through
Frontotemporal Degeneration

Deborah G. Thelwell

For Alan and Madison Paige
xx

Contents

Acknowledgements vii

"Dance Me to the End of Love" ix

Introduction xiii

Prologue xvii

BEFORE

"The Hills Are Alive..." 1

Southampton 7

Early Days 11

Baby Makes Three, then Four 17

Arizona 23

Palm Desert 29

DURING

Testing, Testing 36

Money, Money, Money 43

Missing in Action 48

Travel Troubles 54

Obsessions 64

Rage, Baby 70

Tragedy 75

Day Tripper 81

My Husband, the Five-Year-Old Boy 88

Open Wide Please 98

Incarceration. 103

Mesa 111

One-to-One 117

Maryland, Marriage, and Moving 122

Off to Maravilla. 128

Chopin and Changin'. 133

Last Dance 136

Hospice. 142

Final days 146

The Music's Stopped, It's Time to go Home 152

"Stars". 159

AFTER

The Music Plays On, but the Dancers Have Left the Floor 160

Acknowledgements

I have so much love, gratitude, and respect for
our wonderful sons, Christopher and Adam, and their exceptional families who
faced every challenge with love, strength, and respect for their dad.

To David and Lydia Thelwell, Susan and John Watson, and Lorraine and Glenn
Roberts whose selfless, unconditional love for so long made Alan feel so very
proud and loved.

To my mother, Dorothy Manley, whose endowed strength
carried me through our journey.

To my amazing coworkers, Kathi Zarubi, JoLynn Schick,
Carrie Richer, Nema McElveen, and Linda Duncan to name but a very few of
the dozens at Scottsdale Healthcare who carried me through some of the darkest of days when it was all I could do to just show up at work.

To Dr. Geri Hall, Dr. Maribeth Gallagher, Rebekah Wilson,
and all the members of the
FTD Support Group at Banner Alzheimer's Institute, Phoenix, Arizona.

To the staff at Maravilla Care Center, Phoenix, for their undying,
selfless love and care for others.
To the staff of Hospice of the Valley, Phoenix, Arizona,
for their understanding and kindness.

And last, but not least,
To the many friends and family who supported us from near and far. They are
too numerous to mention each of them individually, but of special note are
Bob and Carole Glass, John and Amanda Marlor, our many friends in
Los Angeles, and everyone all over the world who wrote messages to us on
www.caringbridge.com.

If I left you out, I apologize. The good guys know who they are.

Love always,

Debbie and Alan

xxx

"Dance Me to the End of Love"

Dance me to your beauty with a burning violin
Dance me through the panic 'til I'm gathered safely in
Lift me like an olive branch and be my homeward dove
Dance me to the end of love
Dance me to the end of love

Oh, let me see your beauty when the witnesses are gone
Let me feel you moving like they do in Babylon
Show me slowly what I only know the limits of
Dance me to the end of love
Dance me to the end of love

Dance me to the wedding now, dance me on and on
Dance me very tenderly and dance me very long
We're both of us beneath our love, we're both of us above
Dance me to the end of love,
Dance me to the end of love

Dance me to the children who are asking to be born
Dance me through the curtains that our kisses have outworn
Raise a tent of shelter now, though every thread is torn
Dance me to the end of love

Dance me to your beauty with a burning violin
Dance me through the panic till I'm gathered safely in
Touch me with your naked hand or touch me with your glove.
Dance me to the end of love,
Dance me to the end of love,
Dance me to the end of love.

—Leonard Cohen

The Dance

Our Journey Through
Frontotemporal Degeneration

Introduction

My story is not really a memoir per se. Certainly not a "misery memoir." (Well, I hope not, anyway.) It is not a self-help book. Nor does it contain advice about what to do if you have someone in your life who has Frontotemporal Degeneration (FTD). You may pick up a few tips here and there about how I handled certain behaviors. But my main purpose is to tell our story and to expose this horrific disease for what it really is: a life-stealing bastard.

The story is a loving tribute to the thirty-eight years I spent with a funny, kind, and generous man. He was not just those things of course. He was annoying, stubborn, and argumentative too. Oh, and did I mention irritating?

But I loved him, and he loved me.

I hope you will indulge me as I talk about our early lives together. The tales serve to illustrate how "normal" our lives were. Normal, but at the same time unique. As is everyone's life. We all think our lives are special, but by describing how we met, married, and lived, I hope to somehow paint a picture for you. I know no one ever loved Alan the same way I did and still do. I know no one loves you or yours like you do. I hope you will find my reflections and narrative interesting.

When I was in nursing school my tutor, Monica, gifted me two of the most important lessons of my life. The first was "When in a horrible situation, which seems untenable or especially difficult, ask yourself 'What's the worst that can happen?'"

The second was "Being a nurse is not what you do, it's who you are."

I have carried these two philosophies with me for over twenty years. Little did I know then how important they would become to me.

In the months since Alan's death, as so many grieving widows, widowers, parents, and children have written before me, my perspective on life has changed. I am more mellow and thoughtful. I learn things from places I never would have looked before.

My own emotions are apparent, but anyone in a similar situation, (for none are the same) may identify with some of them. I share how our story unfolded to perhaps offer a point of reference, maybe even a little reassurance for the partners and caregivers who find themselves in this surreal situation. People who never foresaw such drama entering their lives and taking over. It sounds like a cliché, but it's not so much that you never think it will happen to you or yours, more that you don't even really think about it at all. You will almost certainly get through or around the horror, but perhaps never *over* it. There's a real difference, and only a few people understand that.

I don't like to think of what happened to Alan as a tragedy. He lived for almost fifty-eight years and loved his life. The term "tragedy" should be reserved for events such as losing a child, a school shooting, or the disastrous effects of an earthquake or hurricane. What happened to our family was that we were forced to experience life in an unusual way. We are forever changed by Alan's illness and will never be quite the same again. We are still close, loving, and devoted, but with a large piece of the fabric of our little tight-knit group missing.

I hope that each of you will feel something from reading our story, even if it's only that you hate it. I know rejection is not the fearsome thing I once thought it was. I hope perhaps someone can identify with some or all of it and be comforted by the fact that these two not-so-ordinary people went through the experience of FTD, and one came out the other side. Battered and bruised but still going. I have found solace in my solitude, choosing to embrace my own company and my memories. James Altucher calls it "time-travelling." I'm not sure it's healthy, but it feels good to me right now.

I have my work. I venture out from time to time, mostly with my family. I have tried a few new experiences. Sometimes being with people who don't know your story is refreshing.

But I always come back to my family. The family Alan and I made, shared, and loved.

I wish you love and strength if you are on a journey of your own.

Thank you for sharing ours.

Prologue

WHITE-KNUCKLE RIDE FOR MY BIRTHDAY

He spent the whole thirty-minute journey raging and yelling at me. Banging on the window of the car door with his fist. It was as if he knew something was happening. I think he was very scared, as was I. I held on to the steering wheel with white knuckles as he screamed abuse at me with clenched fists, shouting, "Want thump you! Hate you!"

I was trying to figure out what I would do if he started hitting me while I was driving on the freeway. I decided I would pull over to the shoulder. Maybe someone would stop to help me. But then I thought if I stopped, he might get out of the car and walk into the traffic. No good choice to be had, really.

The screaming continued. I drove frantically along, trying to ignore the fury and danger, the fear and disbelief.

We arrived at the hospital in one piece but very frazzled. He would not get out of the car. I was about to call for a hospital security officer to help me when he suddenly changed his mind after my begging and pleading to let the dentist help him.

He was so scared, vulnerable, afraid, and untrusting of me.

We arrived at the locked door of the secure unit on the third floor, and he began to look at me suspiciously. The door was opened, and we were escorted into a large room.

On the way through we could see the other patients in the hall. Some were elderly, confused people, and some were younger people with obvious psychiatric issues. There was an air of being on the knife edge of something dramatic. Something on that fine line between sanity and insanity, between understanding and unknowing.

To imagine my husband in such an institution filled me with dread. I had imagined that day many times. But the sights, smells, and sounds of an inpatient psychiatric unit are hard for anyone to take.

My imaginings came nowhere close to the reality.

BEFORE

One

"THE HILLS ARE ALIVE..."

*I*t's green. That's the first thing you think as you fly over Stockport to land at Manchester Airport. Green. Well, that's because it rains 300 days of the year. (This is not a meteorological fact, just my opinion).

I shouldn't put it down too much or at all really. Stockport was my home for thirty-seven of the first forty-three years of my life. I grew up there from the age of six.

Stockport was Alan's fourth place of residence in the first three years of his life. His father, Bill, was in the army, the Royal Signals. The family spent the first few years of Alan's life posted in Tripoli, Libya, where he was born, and Germany. The final posting was at Catterick Camp where the family waited for Bill's discharge and subsequent return to Stockport. Despite the mobility of army life, the family always thought of Stockport as their home, and they still do.

Arriving in Stockport at the age of three, I'm sure Alan didn't care about its history or geographical attributes. But he came to be very proud of both as he aged. Patriotic and loyal, he loved his hometown, but he also loved to travel and compare.

In 1974, with the disco era in full swing in Stockport, the paths of two people crossed, not once but twice. For those eighteen- and nineteen-year-olds, life was full of promise and adventurous prospects. Boys still asked girls to dance in those days. The girls either made their night or left them dejected and embarrassed based on their response.

Alan was nineteen, travelling the world in the Royal Merchant Navy. He rubbed shoulders with the rich and famous on what was then the world's largest cruise liner: Cunard's Queen Elizabeth 2 (QE2). He would regale his friends (and anyone else who would listen) and try to impress the girls with his tales of travelling the world and serving Jackie Onassis, David Bowie, and rich Arab oil sheikhs aboard the famous ship.

I was eighteen and had recently moved back home to my parents' house after trying my hand at working away for the summer and living with friends in Liverpool for a while. I was working in a job I hated in a department store in Manchester selling wigs. (I know, sounds thrilling.)

I was, I suppose, quite naive in some ways. Although I had been working full time since I was sixteen, and I had lived elsewhere from my hometown and my parents, I took a lot for granted. Looking back, I was totally unaware of much that was going on around me. I just focused on my life and my needs and what I wanted to do. Miss Independence. Your typical selfish teenager really.

Although I had a bit of a reputation as a headstrong, independent person, especially in school, I was actually quite unsure of myself. My outward "confidence" was mere bravado. I would second guess myself all the time and rarely confided in anyone about my real feelings or insecurities. I just used my big mouth to cover up what I was really thinking and feeling.

Our paths had first crossed in 1972 when I was sixteen. My friend Jill and I thought it was cool to hang out in the town center, sitting on the department store windowsills in Mersey Square in the evening when the shops were closed. The surrounding Victorian buildings always seemed to look down disapprovingly on the rowdy crowd.

The attraction there, of course, was a large group of boys and girls between the ages of fourteen and seventeen. Those in-between ages where you don't want to hang out at home with your parents like a kid, and you're not old enough to go to the pub for a drink (although the latter was not for the lack of trying).

The boys had scooters. The Vespa kind. They would park in a line across the front of the shopping precinct, revving their tinny engines, showing off to the girls, and comparing mechanical notes with the boys. The boys dressed neatly in parkas, Ben Sherman shirts, Wrangler or Levi jeans, and Doc Martens boots or

Royals shoes (brogues). They wore their hair short or shaved. The term "skinheads" meant something completely different in those days. We had no time for the "greasers" or "rockers."

Lots of the girls (including me) had short hair, feathered at the sides and back, and often they wore similar clothes to the boys. Two-tone suits, Crombie coats, jeans or Tonick pants with braces and Doc Martens or monkey boots.

Alan or "Thelly,"was one the popular members of the group. A guy everyone liked being around and who was always at the center of everything. The style of music and dancing that was popular with our crowd at that time was something called Northern Soul. Northern Soul is a type of African-American music that is rooted in a mixture of blues, soul, and the Tamla-Motown sound. Mitch Ryder's "Breakout," Johnny Johnson, and Chairman of the Board were all favorites. It was a very (eponymous) northern phenomenon. There were special kinds of dances associated with that style of music, which was a kind of forerunner to the break dancing of the 1980s. The dancing was mostly done by the boys, with the girls grouped around the dance floor admiring the acrobatics exerted by the objects of their desire (Sigh).

Alan and his friends were always good to watch, spinning and back flipping, turning and twisting as they moved to the strong beats. Our favorite places, Blazes and County Club, were packed with teenagers eager to show off their talents to one another. It was a community built from several smaller communities. The surrounding areas were rivals in every sense of the word. Teenagers dating and fighting with each other just like in every other small town in the world. Some of the clubs in Manchester and Stoke would have "all-nighters." The boys would head out of Stockport and dance all night at The Twisted Wheel, The Torch, and Wigan Casino, often fueled by amphetamines.

My friend Jill and I, being only sixteen, never made it to one of those nights, but it always sounded so daring and rebellious to us.

We tried to go once, each of us telling our parents we were staying at the other's house overnight. But the one we planned to go to was cancelled. We were devastated. Well, that's a little dramatic, but we were sixteen after all. Jill quite fancied Alan, but I never saw the attraction of Thelly and thought he was bigheaded and flashy. (Well, a girl can change her mind, can't she?) Our paths were not to cross again for another couple of years, and Alan later said he was not even aware of my existence.

So much for love at first sight.

In 1973 Alan secured his prestigious job on the Queen Elizabeth 2. He always looked back proudly on that time as a very happy part of his life, and he travelled and saw places that most people of our generation could only dream of in those days: islands in the Pacific, Australia, Scandinavia, Europe, and the Americas.

On May 3, 1974, I was out for girl's night with my friend Elaine at the current town-center hotspot, Sergeant Pepper's (yes, like the Beatles song). We were having a great time dancing, flirting, drinking, and generally being eighteen-year-olds. I was wearing a new outfit. A pink, fluffy, halter-neck top; high-waisted, wool, herringbone pants; and shoes with three-inch platforms. Ah, the sartorial delights of the 1970s.

"WHERE IT ALL BEGAN—SGT. PEPPERS NIGHTCLUB, STOCKPORT, 1974."

I felt good. I had no idea this would be the night that would change my life forever. Enter Thelly and his mate, Chris. Alan was wearing a burgundy, velvet jacket, a large-collared shirt open at the neck, and black pants with his platform shoes (it was the '70s, remember?). His light brown hair was a little longer than I remembered with a slight curl at the ends. He was a short guy, five feet seven inches, but he always seemed tall to me. (I'm five feet nothing). He had a big personality, which belied his often-diminished self-confidence. The thing that struck me most of all was his smile. He had a big smile.

Chris was a good friend of Elaine's and mine who lived in the same village, Marple. Elaine and I had been neighbors since we were six years old and remain friends to this day. Elaine did show a little interest in Alan, so being the competitive spirit I am, I decided I would beat her to it by flirting a little myself. Coincidentally, Elaine is my friend Jill's cousin. It must run in the family.

Now, here's where the story gets a little confusing. Alan would have you believe that he was actually on a date with another girl at the time and that I completely ignored her and asked him to dance. I remember it a little differently, but hey, it was almost forty years ago. So, let's just say we danced and that was the beginning of our life together.

We spent every day I wasn't working and every evening of the next three weeks together. I can remember walking down from the railway station in Manchester on my way to work one morning as if I were floating on air. I felt like Julie Andrews in the opening scene of *The Sound of Music*. My heart wanted to sing every song it heard. I wanted to run up to everyone I met and shout at the top of my lungs, "I love Alan Thelwell!" Like everyone newly in love, I thought that no one had ever felt like that before. I was deliriously happy. By the time Alan returned to his ship, we were deeply in love and could not imagine spending our lives with anyone else, and we were right. We spent the rest of his life together.

So maybe it was love at second sight?

Our dance lasted until September 17, 2012. Almost thirty-eight years. But the last few years were syncopated to a different beat. We had lots of fun and a few tears along the way, but we always danced in step and only stepped on each other's toes once or twice. As we moved towards forty years together, our dance was interrupted by something that wanted to cut in.

The intruder that buried itself in Alan's head was determined to push him out to make way for another. Someone I didn't know, and often didn't like, but who became more familiar in the last five years of Alan's life.

Two

SOUTHAMPTON

*W*hen Alan left Stockport to return to the ship in June of 1974, I returned to my boring job at the wig shop. I caught up with my friends and generally mooched about, pining for my newfound love. The ship had gone on a short hop to New York—five days out and five days back. So by the time the ten days had gone by, I had decided on that Friday afternoon I would just go down to Southampton and meet the ship and surprise Alan.

Ah, the impetuosity of youth.

After work I went to the bank, drew out what little money I had (selling and grooming wigs did not pay well), and caught the train to Southampton, arriving at about 10:00 p.m. I got a taxi from the station and spent the next four hours quayside on number thirty-eight to thirty-nine.

There was a man waiting for the ship too. A salty, old sailor-type returning from his shore leave. He kindly offered me one of his salmon-paste sandwiches (yuck) after I fainted from hunger, because I hadn't eaten since that morning. The sandwich made me throw up, so we just hung around in silence together (well really, what could he say?) and waited it out. Luckily it was June, and it wasn't cold or raining. Three hours later, at two in the morning, QE2 sailed gracefully into her dock, and the passengers and some of the crew disembarked. My newfound sea dog, sailor friend disappeared onto the ship, promising he would try to find

Alan, but I didn't hold out much hope for that. Clearly, I hadn't thought the whole process through.

I asked several people coming down the gangway if they knew Alan, but I didn't have much success. I later discovered there were over a thousand crew members. Eventually I asked someone who said they didn't know him, but thought he knew where Alan worked, so off the kind chap went in search of my love. Alan came off the ship a little while later, sleepy-eyed and curious as to whom "some girl waiting for you on the quayside" could be. He was delighted to see me, and we went off to a very nice hotel in Southampton and spent the next three days together.

After that, I only ever went to Southampton on prearranged visits. We used to stay in a small bed-and-breakfast run by "the Colonel" and his lady wife. They were great fun, but seemed very old to us, although they were probably only in their forties at the time. I wore a fake wedding ring and we called ourselves "Mr. and Mrs. Thelwell" as it was not really proper in those days for couples to stay in hotel rooms if they were not married (I know, it seems so archaic now). We listened to Elton John's "Bennie and the Jets" and danced to The Hughes Corporation's "Rock the Boat." We laughed and loved. We were young and carefree.

When his father died in November of 1974, Alan's mother had to call him on the ship-to-shore radio via Cunard, which was only ever used in cases of great emergency. It took five more days for him to find a flight home from the Caribbean islands, and he arrived one day too late for the funeral. I met him at the train station, not knowing what to say. It was like a scene out of a black-and-white movie from the 1940s, *Brief Encounter* or *Mrs. Miniver*. Me standing on the platform waiting for the train, him hanging out of the train window anxiously looking for me. No romantic steam though. I had no idea what to say to him. It was the first of many sad family occasions we would share together.

The next two years were spent with Alan sailing around the world on the QE2 and me settling into a new job at a sportswear manufacturer after having left the wig department (thank goodness). Alan came home on leave quite frequently, except for 1975, when the QE2 sailed off on her maiden world voyage. For ninety-two days they visited the Far East, the Pacific Islands, North and South America. In those days without the Internet, cellphones, or even easy international phone calls, we relied on the appropriately nicknamed "snail mail."

During those long trips, I had the ship's itinerary, and I would carefully plan out what date I had to mail my letter in order for it to get to the next port before Alan and the ship did. It usually got there in time, and like a scene from *M.A.S.H.*, the crew would wait excitedly for the mail bag to arrive with their letters and parcels from their loved ones back home. I still have all the letters he wrote over that time, along with the ones I sent to Alan, which he kept too. Those flimsy, blue airmail envelopes with the striped edges seem so old-fashioned now. It's strange to look back at who we were then and compare us to who we became. Nowadays I read the letters with tears in my eyes. It's as if the writers of those love letters were two entirely different people. So much in our lives was so good. Those early times were a good precursor of the many happy times we were to share in the years that followed.

AN EVENING IN "THE PIG"—QE2'S CREW BAR, 1975

In June 1975, right after Alan's return from the world cruise, we celebrated our engagement with a party at my parent's house in Marple. All our friends and family were there, along with some of Alan's shipmates: Steve Wooster, John McKenna, and Mick Farthing. They were people I came to know and love and remain in contact with today.

We were having a rare English heat wave, so the party was outside in the garden. The hit record of the day was "The Hustle." It was what we call in England a *good do*, and everyone had a great time. There were several sore heads the next morning. Alan and I danced until the early hours. We were so much in love and looking forward to a great future together.

After that, Alan sailed off on his trips, and I continued my life and work. Life ticked along. We danced at many more engagement parties, weddings, and christenings as our friends all got their lives in order too. Our crowd from the square was all grown up.

We were married on October 30, 1976. There wasn't really a proposal, more a mutual understanding that it was just what we would do. There was no need to ask. It was a given. By that time we were co-running a business with my parents, so we were married from "the shop" as we called it. Alan's family and some of our friends came to the wedding in a bus. It was a cold, damp October day, but we never noticed the weather. The church bells rang, our friends Chris and Elaine were best man and bridesmaid. Our reception was at a local hotel, 'The Heaton Park'. We danced until dawn. All the boys took off their pants and danced the conga in their underwear while singing, "We are the hot-pant boys!" Dancing was in our blood, and we were all young and reckless.

We honeymooned in a cottage in the Lake District, a beautiful rural area of England. It was early November. It snowed, and we kept cosy in our little cottage. I swear we ate and drank more that week than any other time after that. Every day, we would have a full English breakfast, then morning coffee, and toasted teacakes; lunch; afternoon tea; and a roast dinner in the evening followed by drinks in the local pub and doing what honeymooners do back at the cottage. We returned fat and happy.

So began our married life together. That week we spent in Windermere was blissful. I loved him with all my heart.

I still do.

Three

EARLY DAYS

For the first seven years of our married life we were, by choice, child-less. We married young and had a lot of living to do. We enjoyed one another's company, our friends, and the life we were building together. We were determined to have all the things we wanted. We bought our first house and cars, went on many vacations, spent time with our friends, and, of course, danced until many a dawn.

One of our favorite haunts was Bredbury Hall, a popular local nightclub and hotel. Bredders, as it was known, was open all night and served breakfast in the early hours to those stalwarts like us who danced all through the night and emerged the next morning hungry and energized from the music and dancing. If we left early (2:00 a.m. to 3:00 a.m.), we would go home and eat horribly in-nutritious things in bed. (Ask any Englishman about "chip butties.") We would lie there, snuggled under the covers, in the cold, grey light of dawn in our little flat and talk about the great things we knew were to come for us.

After we left the shop where we lived and worked with my parents, we moved back to Stockport. We lived in a small, ground-floor flat in an old, converted Victorian house with no heating. I did the laundry in a thirdhand washing ma-chine that I had to pull out from its wall to the sink so it could drain into there.

The bathroom was so cold you could see your breath. We would strip-wash in the sink in the kitchen in the mornings and take a bath in the evening when we had time to preheat the bathroom with a space heater. Our upstairs neighbor, Janice, had loud and frequent sex with a succession of boyfriends. We would sit downstairs and laugh at her "don't-care" attitude, even when Alan told her we could hear her.

We weren't materially rich, but we were very happy.

When my parents separated in 1977, I was devastated. I had no idea anything was wrong. They had kept the secret very well. I started to have panic attacks. I couldn't even stand in line in a shop for fear of fainting. Alan was so supportive. When we suddenly had to leave places because of my anxiety, he would always be kind and understanding. If he was irritated with me, he certainly never showed it.

We were able to save and afford my very first trip abroad and on an airplane. We travelled to Crete, the largest of the Greek islands.

For a seasoned traveller like Alan, it was just another trip. But for me, it was the beginning of a lifelong love of travel. I loved everything about that trip: the flight, the sights, the smells, and the history of Crete, the site of one of oldest civilizations in the world. I can remember stepping off the plane and breathing in the hot, dry night air. For a girl from a damp, industrial city like Manchester, it was like a dream. We travelled with our friend Chris and his wife Barbara. I have some great memories of that trip, meeting new friends and sharing new experiences. Even the onset of "Aphrodite's Revenge," a tummy bug that ran rampant through our hotel, didn't spoil the experience for me. I discovered that one of the oldest civilizations in the world also had one of the most primitive sanitation systems.

I was working at a commercial kitchen maintenance company as the office manager (I like a varied work life as you can see), and Alan worked as a sales rep for a hardware supplier. He really liked that job. No one watching over his shoulder. He got to drive around all day in the company car and spend time chatting with people. He never had to "hard sell" anyone. He was so charming and likable; people placed their orders without any pressure.

"ON HOLIDAY, TORQUAY, JULY 1978."

In 1981, we both left our "good" jobs and went to work for a brewery, Bass Charrington. We received extensive training in hospitality management—an extension of the training Alan had received in the Merchant Navy. We learned how to run a pub, restaurant, and hotel and trained as relief managers so we could go in and take over a pub when the manager was on vacation or was fired. Our friends and family thought we were crazy. But it was a way for us to learn the trade so eventually we could fulfill our dream to have our own bar. We travelled week by week throughout our local area, spending a week or two in each place. Some bars were in very rough areas of town. Often the locals would be suspicious of us, but Alan always made friends with the most "shady" of the customers and gained protection for us right away. He was very smart at that. He had a way about him, so that when we left after two or three weeks, we left many new friends behind.

The first pub we went to, The Crown, was in the city center of Manchester. It was slap-bang in the middle of a rough, inner-city housing estate called Hulme. The managers went on vacation and left their dog, Max, a Doberman, as protection for us. The safe was in the bedroom where we slept, there were no carpets on the floors, and we slept with a large machete stuck into the floorboards on each side of the bed at night. Lovely! We were scared and inexperienced. But we got through. We stuck together like glue, knowing that we could always trust one another even if there was no one else.

As it turned out, the customers and staff were wonderful, warm people. We celebrated our fifth wedding anniversary there and were surprised to receive cards and gifts from people we had only just met.

One place was particularly tough. We could not stay there at night, as the suspended manager was still living upstairs. He had been locked out, pending investigation, so we had to travel from our house every day. I took charge of the cooking of the "pub grub" at lunchtime, and Alan managed the bar. The ex-manager was not allowed in the pub. However, he still had contact with the customers and tried to get them to help him persuade the brewery not to fire him. Alan and I would go there in the mornings for opening at 11:00 a.m., drive the fourteen miles home at 3:00 p.m., and then Alan would return alone at 5:00 p.m. ready for the evening session. He was so protective. He would not let me go with him at night, as he knew how rough it was. The pub closed at 11:00 p.m. So, by the time he had cashed up, cleaned up, and was ready to leave, it was usually around midnight.

One night he left the pub, locked the doors, and turned around to find a group of men threatening him and warning him off. They wanted to prove that the resident manager was the only one who could run such a tough place. Alan managed to run to our little MG sports car which, unfortunately, would not start immediately. He spent several seconds sweating until finally the engine turned over, and he sped off.

We went to several places like that. It was common for all the customers who had been barred by the previous manager to come back in, as we would never know who was barred. Another time, Alan was assaulted late at night outside the pub we were managing. His face was slashed with the edge of a sharpened credit card. On our first day at another place, a group of customers picked up and threw the pool table through the large picture window at the front of the pub. Then they had the nerve to complain the next day that there was no pool table for them to play on!

One day at that pub a customer said, "I'm coming over this bar and taking the money out of the till, and there's nothing you can do about it."

Alan's response was to pull out the baseball bat he kept under the bar and say, "Oh yeah?"

The guy left the pub and never came back. For a short guy, Alan could really be quite fierce! "Jack Russell Terrier/Napoleon" complex, I guess.

Another time we got word that the pub we were managing was going to be robbed after hours, so we sat after closing with several of the regulars who were armed with baseball bats and other weapons. As I said before, Alan always made friends with the most infamous customers as a form of protection for us. Once word got around that we were under the protection of "Frankie" (who had his leather trench coat specially tailored to include an interior pocket for his sawed-off shotgun), we were never bothered again. All it cost us was a few extra drinks after hours.

Our relationship was very strong, and we always made decisions together. We were a united front in some very harsh situations.

In 1982, because of our experience in the hospitality business, Alan was asked by the manager of a local bar that we went to sometimes if Alan would cover for him while he went on vacation. The Three Shires Wine Bar was located in the center of Stockport, and the manager, Nick, assured Alan he would be back in three or four weeks. The month went really well. Alan established a great relationship with the owner, Mike, and when six weeks went by and there was no sign of Nick returning from his "vacation," Mike asked Alan to take over as permanent manager.

The arrangement worked very well, and we were successful in making The Shires one of the top places in town. The place is a small, sixteenth-century building built in Tudor times as the townhouse of the Legh family. It is very compact, so when it was busy, it was a case of "one out, one in." On a Friday night there was a line outside the door as people waited for their turn to come in. We were the first bar in town to start "happy hour." The New Romantics music was all the rage, and we would go clubbing after hours with our staff and friends and dance until dawn.

The local newspaper dubbed The Shires "the place to see and be seen." Alan was quite the local celebrity and loved every minute of it. His innovative and creative ideas sparked success and great memories.

We signed the paperwork to purchase the business from Mike on September 17, 1983, the night our first child, Christopher, was born. And so began the next chapter of our lives as business partners and parents.

We were dancing with joy.

"PROUD DADDY"

Four

BABY MAKES THREE, THEN FOUR

y the time Christopher came along, Alan and I knew each other very well and we had lived a little, so to speak. We were busy running our business and having a new baby, but we juggled everything well. I surprised myself by really enjoying being a stay-at-home mother, and it wasn't long before our second son Adam was on his way. It probably seemed to onlookers that we had it all: a successful business, our own house, two kids, and our Doberman, Jasper.

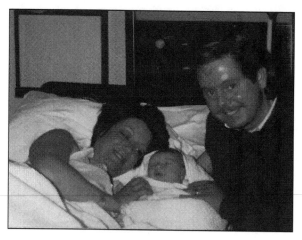

"ANOTHER BOY—YIPPEE!"

Alan loved his boys. He was so proud of them. He would enjoy showing them off to his friends, and he bragged about their accomplishments. He coached Adam's soccer team, and I would go along to Chris's matches, as they played on different teams on the same day of the week. We have some great memories of family times—summer holidays, Christmases—all the things that families do together.

Although there was a lot of love in their house, Alan did not receive the same kind of encouragement and support from his parents that he was always eager to provide for his own children. Don't get me wrong, he was not "super dad." His whole world did not revolve around his children. In fact, sometimes I wished he would spend a little more time with us. But he was, as in all things, loyal, true, reliable, and loving to his family.

In the years before the boys came along, we had both been able to go out and enjoy time with our friends in our wine bar or a different place on Alan's rare days off. Once I was not around so much, however, Alan's social circle changed, and he spent a lot of time with the local business people who frequented our bar both during the day and in the evening. The Shires was still the "in" place to go, and Alan reveled in the popularity and attention. He and his friends worked hard, played hard, and drank hard. They were affluent and successful and they loved their "Sundance"—their nickname for Alan. He spent long hours away from home ensuring the success of the bar. (Well, he would call it that. Others may say it was just a great excuse to drink and hang out with his friends!).

Alan was happy, the business was successful, and I felt that I had got those partying days out of my system. I was content to be at home and enjoy our kids. Alan enjoyed spending time with his family as much as he enjoyed spending time with his friends, and he afforded me the same freedom. He often did his share of babysitting while I went out with friends or his sister, Lorraine, and enjoyed myself too. Our love was solid. We both felt secure but never took it for granted.

We sold the wine bar in 1986 to a friend, Alan Harvey, and continued to frequent the place with our family and friends. Alan focused his efforts on a new role in real estate, working with friends Ronnie and Jeff. He enjoyed several successful years with them before opening his own brokerage, Terraced Homes. Again, he loved the sociality and freedom of his work: meeting new people, talking with them, and being out in the world without constraints. No nine-to-five for him.

In 1989 Alan's brother, David, moved to Los Angeles. Alan and David had become very close as David grew into adulthood. Despite the nine-year age gap, they were the best of friends, and it hit Alan hard when David left. There was still no Internet at that point, but there were many long, late-night, international phone calls between the brothers. One (or both) of them was usually a little worse for wear.

In 1991, being unable to stand the distance any longer, Alan flew out to Los Angeles for a visit with his baby brother. He was so proud of what David had achieved. When he came home, Alan bragged vicariously about the life David and Lydia were making for themselves. I think at that point, Alan had subconsciously decided it might be something we could do too. He mentioned it when he returned, but we put the idea on the back burner until we had a better means of being able to emigrate legally and securely as we had our boys to think about too.

"PORTO COLON, SUMMER 1993"

19

In 1993 I enrolled in nursing school. We had made a fairly comfortable life for our boys and ourselves. We had our own home. Alan was running his business in finance and real estate, and he was able to be at home with the boys when I was at the hospital or in class. He coached Adam's football team on the weekends. As the boys grew and became more independent, Alan and I got a little freedom back, and with the help of Grandma, (my mother, Dorothy) we were able to start going out (dancing, of course) together and with our friends a little more.

During that time, Alan, as always, worked hard at whatever he was doing, be it finance, real estate, or car sales. He was very successful at using his personality to engage with people and always learning something new to keep himself engaged in whatever it was that had his attention at the time. Learning Spanish, real estate law, or the nuances of the mortgage and pension industry. He had a high school education, never went to college, but he was intelligent, articulate, and resourceful. He was a regular at the gym, ate well, ran, played golf, and generally kept himself fit and healthy. Before he went to visit David in 1991, he had spent a whole year cigarette and alcohol free, lost weight, and generally felt good about himself.

We all flew out to Los Angeles in June of 1995 for David and Lydia's wedding. It was a wonderful time, and I think it was the final catalyst in deciding to make the move to the States. We began making preliminary plans as to how we could achieve our dream.

"BROTHERLY LOVE"

When I graduated from nursing school in 1996, Alan was extremely proud. He was so supportive while I was a student nurse and encouraged me to do whatever I wanted. He took care of the boys so I could study and was always interested in what I was doing.

In 1997 Alan and I finally made the decision to emigrate. It was difficult leaving our friends and family, but we both felt it was the best move for the boys and us. I had my nursing, and Alan took classes to earn his badges, which would enable him to officially coach football in the United States.

David and Lydia were still living in Los Angeles where we had visited. We liked the United States, and we thought it would be a good time to provide the boys with more opportunity than they might have had in England.

We began the process in January 1998, attending an open house given by a recruitment company that employed nurses from English-speaking countries like the United Kingdom, Australia, and South Africa. Then in July of that year, after attending classes and workshops offered by the company, I flew to Savannah, Georgia, to take my nursing licensing exams. I was gone for five days. It was my first ever time away from my family since the boys were born. It was strangely exciting, but a little nerve-racking being away from them all, especially Alan. It felt strange being a single woman travelling alone. I don't think I had ever done that before. Not on a plane, anyway.

Once I had my American nursing license, we just had to wait for the US immigration services to do its part. We sold our house and furniture and moved into a rented house close to my work and the boys' school. Our belongings were packed, with some things going to storage, some moved into the new house, to await a final date to emigrate.

It was a strange time. As if we only had half a life. We were in a different house, and we had one foot out of the door at work. We had so many leaving parties; I think people began to wonder if we were ever actually going to go. It was a hard, snowy winter. Our rented house didn't feel like home. Even though we had our usual Christmas tree and decorations, it was all so surreal.

In November, I successfully interviewed in London along with hundreds of other nurses for a job in Phoenix, Arizona that would begin just as soon as the immigration paperwork could be completed. All four of us were summoned to

London for our interview with the US Immigration Department in Grosvenor Square on March 18, 1999. We were told we were approved to travel to and enter the United States.

We spent the last few days staying with our friends Steve and Jane before finally leaving England behind on March 30, 1999.

We were doing it!

We were moving to America to dance stateside.

"LEAVING PARTY. ONE OF MANY!"

Five

ARIZONA

*W*hen we arrived at Sky Harbor Airport, Phoenix, our "meet-and-greet" person, Carrie, eventually showed up at the airport over an hour late, leaving us standing at the airport tired, anxious, jet-lagged and surrounded by all our belongings.

Welcome to the United States!

The next day Carrie came to pick us up, along with another couple, Gillian and Wayne, who had arrived from England the previous day. Carrie drove us around, frequently getting lost, much to all our amusement and irritation. That first week we had to furnish and settle into our apartment, go to the social security office to get our cards, get the boys into school, open a bank account, and obtain driver's licenses. It was a busy few days. We arrived on Tuesday night, and Gillian and I had to be in orientation at our new jobs at a downtown hospital on Thursday, which meant that Alan and the boys were responsible for doing lots of those things without me. I think it was a great time for them to bond in adversity. They only had each other, and they had to figure things out together.

It was emotionally draining and stressful moving to a new country and culture. As has been said, "Britain and America—two countries divided by a common language."

Our sons were fourteen and fifteen, and they had to adjust quickly to new schools, friends, and neighborhood. They settled reasonably well, as did I in my new job at a downtown hospital. It was more difficult for Alan. He had to find his own job and friends. We had no car at first, and Phoenix is lacking in a good public transport system. Luckily our apartment was within walking distance of several places.

For all of us nurses who started there over a period of about three months, there were huge changes to get used to, both for us and our new coworkers. There were many evenings when Gillian, another English nurse, Christine, and I drove home together and one or more of us was in tears. The stress of so much change in a very short space of time took its toll on all of us. There was a great pressure on those of us with families to be successful. Most of the wives who were nurses were the breadwinners for their families.

I can remember one evening when Alan came home, and the boys and I were sitting on the floor of the balcony of our apartment crying. Homesickness had got the better of us. Alan joined in too. We were and are very close. Any kind of upset or turmoil in our lives affects us all equally. There was an element of culture shock for us all. For Alan more than the rest of us it seemed. It was hard for him to start over. But after a while, he too found new friends, enjoyed his new job at the golf course, found a bar to frequent, and settled down.

To his great pride, Alan also managed to find a position doing something he loved: coaching football. By networking with other ex-pat Brits, he got a job with the largest, most successful youth soccer club in Arizona, Sereno. Then later, he set up his own teams in another part of the valley. It was heaven to him: the golf course in the mornings, an afternoon nap, and then he was off to football in the late afternoons and evenings.

Alan loved the golf course. It provided two of the things he loved most in life: talking with people and sports. He always said it was the best job he ever had. He was outdoors all day, there was free golf and practice, and he hung out with his friend, Gene, sneaking in a few holes on the back nine when they were supposed to be mowing the greens, moving the pins, or whatever. It was an early start, 4:00 a.m., but he was home by 1:00 p.m. with the afternoon to himself. In the evenings he worked at the soccer club in Scottsdale. He loved being so involved with the teams and the kids. So two of his favorite pastimes became work, and he got paid for it. Imagine that.

The next few years were spent adjusting to our new lives, moving into and out of our apartment, and finding jobs and schools for the boys. Between March and July of 2000, my father died; Christine and three other nurses were involved in a serious car accident in which one of them was killed; we bought a house; and our youngest son, Adam, was involved in a near-fatal car accident in which he was seriously injured.

The experience of almost losing a child was one I would not wish upon my worst enemy. Adam had multiple skull fractures, one of which severed an artery in his temple, which led to bleeding in his brain. He required emergency surgery to drain the blood and repair the fractures. The first twenty-four hours were sheer hell. Neither Alan nor I slept at all. We sat, stood, cried, and yelled during those long hours in the ICU waiting room. Finally the surgeon came out to tell us that Adam was doing well, but he was on a ventilator, and we would see what tomorrow would bring.

Alan could not bear to see our son in such a state. He would often leave the room to just go and sit alone in the waiting area. It was too painful for him to watch. I stood looking on, wondering if Adam would ever wake up again and if so, what would his mental condition be?

Alan and I clung to one another, physically and emotionally. Not knowing was the worst part. We were alternately angry and tearful. Fear was the driving force. But we had always handled adversity together. We found courage in one another. We drew strength from the great love we had for each other and our children. We stood and held hands, clinging to one another for support. Fortunately, Adam made a full recovery over time, but that twelve-month period of 2000 was incredibly stressful. I was so glad when the New Year came around.

My father's death also had a huge impact on all of us, but of course, it took its toll mainly on me. Being so far away and unable to help, I could only listen helplessly to reports from my brother of my dad's decline due to lung cancer. His last weeks were excruciating. Alan was, as ever, very supportive and understanding. It was just another ordeal for us to face together. There was never any question that he would be there to give me what I needed: love, support, and comfort.

We moved into our new house in March of 2000, one year after we arrived in Phoenix. Adam came out of hospital the day before we moved and spent the first few days in our new house in a daze due to his concussion. Alan joked when we moved in that he was never moving again. Six times in fifteen months was more than enough! He said that he would stay in the house until he died, and then we could bury him in the backyard. How (almost) prophetic that joke turned out to be.

Our house is a great place, spacious and comfortable, and we enjoyed it to the full. We had our own pool, which was Alan's pride and joy. We had friends over almost every weekend to swim, barbecue, drink, and generally hang out. Other times at night, Alan and I would swim and skinny-dip together, listening to Crowded House's "Better Be Home Soon." When I listen to it now, it takes me right back to those one hundred degree nights lying on our sun beds in the dark with all the yard lights off, drinking wine and staring at the stars. Sometimes we would even fall asleep out there. We would look at the constellations in the clear night sky through a pair of antique binoculars Alan had brought from England. We relished the hot, dry air and marveled at how lucky we were. We would talk about anything and everything and generally put the world to rights. It was a very happy time.

I need to clarify here that our life was never "idyllic." We had our arguments and falling-outs just like any other couple. Our kids acted out, and we would disagree about how to handle them, about money, about who worked the hardest, about drinking too much. One or the other of us would storm out of the room, the house, the street. We would come back a little later when we had simmered down and laugh at our foolishness. But there was never a suggestion that any of it would affect our love for one another. That was it. We had what we had, and that was it. It never occurred to either of us that it could be any different. It was just natural and unforced.

My sister-in-law, Lydia, and I have often discussed how we grew up in similar families. There was always unconditional love. No matter what you said or did, love was never on the table to be removed if you did something wrong. Disapproval and punishment perhaps, but never was love taken away. Amazingly, although David and Alan had a different experience of family love than Lydia and me, the ability to give and experience deep and unshakeable love was and is part of them. Although the unconditional part came into question at times, I think they both learned a lot from Lydia and me.

Alan worked as hard as ever during our early years in Phoenix. Always in "people-type" jobs, such as greenskeeper at the golf course, football coaching, and later, car sales. He loved that job. It was another job where he got to hang out with other guys, meet new people, and make money. He was settled and very successful there for over two years and made some great friends. It was there that he met his good friend Bob Glass and introduced me to Bob's wife, Carole. Both remain great friends. They were very supportive when we needed them the most. We spent many wonderful times with Bob and Carole and their family. We attended their daughter's wedding and spent Thanksgivings and other holidays together. Alan and Bob played golf and enjoyed each other's company enormously.

"LAS VEGAS 2002"

In 2003 the old "itchy feet" returned, and Alan started talking about moving closer to David in Los Angeles. The boys were grown but not quite independent. So it was agreed that we would move to California, to a midway point between Los Angeles and Phoenix. We decided upon Palm Desert where we would spend the next two years. We left the boys at the house, and Bob helped us move into our new condo.

Our dance was about to take on a different beat.

Six

PALM DESERT

We knew a couple of people in Palm Desert before we moved in. I got a job in the ICU at one of the local hospitals, and Alan started working for a friend, Ian, who owned a chain of shoe repair stores in town.

Alan had originally successfully interviewed for a job at a local car dealership, as he'd planned to continue in the work he had enjoyed in Phoenix. But once we arrived, he said he did not want to do that. He wanted to "try something new." I think his confidence was beginning to ebb a little. Outside his comfort zone he was afraid to be in a situation where he did not know anyone. In hindsight, that was probably the very beginning of our long journey through dementia, which continued for the next seven years. Things that started happening then now seem to have been indicative of what was to come. Of course, we were completely unaware of that at the time.

For the next two years, never realizing anything was wrong, Alan and I had a vacation lifestyle. In the evenings he coached football, his passion. He worked with Ian in the shop for a year and then, after a falling-out with Ian's business partner, his wife Dee Dee, Alan quit. He then had a succession (I lost count but at least four) of jobs, which were short-lived, sometimes only lasting a few hours. He served in a diner (the owner was "an idiot"), and then he tried window cleaning (he couldn't stand heights). And then he wanted to work at the hospital again. He had worked as a transporter temporarily at the hospital where I worked in England while we were waiting for our immigration paperwork to go through. According to Alan, he always left the jobs under his own volition, and it was never his fault. The elusive "they" were always the ones in the wrong.

In 2004 Alan trained as a cardiac monitor technician. The job involves watching several patients' cardiac rhythms at once and informing the nurse if there are changes or potentially dangerous events. It is a complex task, and Alan had to learn and absorb many new skills, including physiology and anatomy, and to recognize cardiac rhythms sent to an observation monitor screen. He also had to pass a basic life-support test so he could perform CPR on someone during a heart attack. Knowing what I know now, I am still amazed he was able to absorb and learn so much new information, since assimilating new things becomes increasingly difficult in frontotemporal degeneration.

After that training, Alan was successful in obtaining a job in the same intensive care unit where I worked, and we worked well together for several months. We worked the night shift and after our three nights, we would have several days off together. It was just like being on vacation. Alan always declared it, "The best place I've ever lived."

Being a resort town, Palm Desert is full of happy, vacationing people for much of the year, so it's a great place to live. It's small so you can walk everywhere, and there are lots of bars and restaurants. We soon made lots of friends and had some good times. Our Sundays at Roc's Firehouse with Roland, Jayme, Nedim, Ian, and Nigel were some of the best times of our lives. I would sing with the band, and we enjoyed our resort lifestyle. Our friends and family visited often, and we had a ball. Of course, many of those times involved alcohol, so it was difficult to know all was not well with Alan.

"MT. JACINTO, PALM SPRINGS, 2003"

We lived as we had in those early days as newlyweds. We loved each other so much I thought it was not possible for anyone else to know what true love was really like. Of course, he drove me crazy sometimes too. He was stubborn, argumentative, and arrogant (remember "flash" Alan from 1974?), but he always listened to me in the end. Even though he would pretend that whatever it was I had persuaded him to do was his idea, I know he adored me, whatever he said or did. In the years to come that sometimes was the only thing that kept me going.

Early in 2005 Alan decided to leave the hospital, as he wanted to go back to Phoenix. "Maybe go back to the golf course."

This is now understandable given that in those early stages of his as-yet-undiscovered dementia he was probably subconsciously looking for something that made him happy and comfortable. He associated working at the golf course or car dealership in Phoenix with those feelings. He also often spoke about going back to England. I always gave credence to his ideas, as I had no clue then as to what was going on in his head. I was a little confused (and irritated) but not enough to suspect anything.

It was during that time that stranger things, the meaning of which subsequently became clearer, began to crop up.

I remember one night, over Alan's fiftieth-birthday weekend, he, David, Lydia, and I had a heated debate about windmills. There is a famous wind farm in Palm Springs. Alan spent a long time trying to convince the three of us that the windmills are powered by electricity and that is what makes them go round. He could not get his head around the fact that they are wind-powered and actually make electricity, rather than use it. We gave up trying to convince him after a long discussion.

While we lived in Palm Desert, I made frequent visits back to Phoenix to visit the boys. Alan joined me sometimes. On one of those occasions, Alan got extremely drunk and belligerent. He threw the boys' friends out of the house, and then insisted that I drive him back to Palm Desert at 2:00 a.m. He was completely out of control, even for an intoxicated person, screaming and yelling. He pushed me on to the bed, because I was trying to stop him from getting in the car and driving himself. Adam intervened, and I gave in and agreed to drive us back to Palm Desert. I spent the three and a half hours almost falling asleep while driving home, the unlit highway hypnotic in its blackness.

I listened to his constant tirade for two hours before he finally fell asleep. We arrived safely back in Palm Desert. It was 5:30 a.m. We did not speak at all, just went straight to bed, and I finally got a little rest at last. I was confused and a little scared. I had seen Alan drunk before, but this experience was way beyond that.

The next day I left the house while Alan was still sleeping, and drove around for four hours before returning to our home in Palm Desert. Back at the condo, Alan was distraught. He had been calling me on my cellphone (which I had ignored). Alan knew something had happened, but he was not sure what. He told me he thought I had left him, and I broke down, telling him, "But where would I go?"

There were places I could have gone of course. Back to Phoenix or to David and Lydia's in Los Angeles. But something stopped me. I could not leave. I would not abandon him. Maybe subconsciously I knew something was wrong.

I think that was the first time in our marriage I had felt so alone and, he was not with me in the true sense of the words. Those were the first signs of what was to come. Alcohol fueling the dementia that was just beginning. So many things became clearer as we advanced along the path on our journey. Alan's propensity for drinking muddied the waters of what was going on in his mind for a long time. Once he was no longer able to hold down a job, I had the opportunity to move back to Phoenix.

In June 2005 we packed up, headed home to Phoenix, and picked up our lives there. We moved back into our house. The boys stayed with us for a short time before finding places of their own. Living with their parents again was not an option in their opinion. I was able to get a job at another hospital; it was a promotion, in fact, and Alan began his quest for that elusive "perfect job" again.

Once more we went through a series of "unsuitable" employers, each one less acceptable to Alan than the last. His resignation or firing often came after just a day or so on a job. Nothing lasted longer than a week or two. At that point, I had no idea that anything was wrong, and I helped Alan with his numerous application forms. There came a time, however, when I realized that he was unable to fill out those forms himself. But he was able to explain it away by saying his computer skills were not up to filling out electronic forms, which many of them had now become. Still, it did not occur to me that anything was wrong. He was only fifty, after all, and fit and healthy in every other respect.

Because of the lack of steady income other than mine, our debts began to accumulate, and we made some very poor choices about our finances. At that point, I still trusted Alan's decision making as much as I always had. Looking back, I should probably have been much more questioning and curious about where our money was going and how it was being managed. But, having no idea what was happening inside Alan's brain, I continued to trust him implicitly. Any suggestion that all was not well was met with denial and defensiveness. I just thought I was being a little suspicious.

One light in our lives at that time was the birth of our first grandson, Sergio Jack, in January of 2006 to Adam and Pamela. Alan was thrilled and spent many hours idolizing the new baby, holding, and playing with him. We both enjoyed many happy hours babysitting and caring for the new addition to our family. However, in the next couple of years, even that joy would turn out to be a source of conflict as any diversion of my attention from Alan caused friction between us. He saw our children and grandchildren as some kind of competition against which he had to vie for attention. That cut me up. I wanted him to share the joy of just having them around, but he felt so threatened by them. They never knew it though. He was always loving and kind to them. Just not to me.

"SERGIO JACK AND HIS GRANDDAD, SUMMER 2006"

That same summer, 2006, we were lucky enough to realize one of our long term dreams —to drive down the Pacific Coast Highway from San Francisco to Los Angeles. With the top down on our car, we traversed the bridge featured in the opening credits of one of our favorite movies from the '70s —*Play Misty for Me*. It was definitely a dream come true for both of us. We had a great time, as always, laughing, people-watching, sitting in a comfortable silence as we drove through Big Sur and Monterey. Places we had only seen in movies, but were now part of our "home" landscape.

In 2007 I began to notice some "word-finding" issues in Alan's speech. During conversation, Alan would insert a word that would begin with the same letter and be of the same length but was completely out of context. For example, "foot" instead of "full." I wondered if he was experiencing transient ischemic attacks (TIAs), which are a sort of "ministroke." Alan was fully aware that it was happening, and he would immediately correct himself. So when I suggested going to see a neurologist for some clarification, he agreed. Even in those early stages, he insisted that if it was "bad news," (a tumor or some other terminal condition), he did not want to know as he "could not handle it."

My old dance partner was beginning to miss a few steps.

DURING

Seven

TESTING, TESTING

In August of 2007 we had an appointment with Dr. R. with whom I worked at the hospital. Dr. R. is an excellent neurologist but could use a little help in the bedside manner department. After a brief discussion and history taking, Dr. R. performed some tests, including the Mini Mental State Examination and a physical exam. The doctor asked Alan to write a sentence, any sentence, on a piece of paper and pass it back to him across the table. Alan wrote, "I like to place golf," substituting the word "place" for "play." He left the paper in front of him and made no attempt to pass it back to Dr. R. He did not follow the doctor's instructions.

Amazingly, just in April of that same year, Alan had studied for his US citizenship interview with the immigration service and passed with flying colors. (Maybe that says more about the naturalization test than Alan's mental state, I'm not sure).

Dr. R. referred Alan to a clinical neuropsychologist at our local specialty center, the Barrow Neurological Institute, for further, more comprehensive assessment. Dr. R. also ordered an MRI to evaluate Alan's brain for any signs of physiological issues, such as a tumor or stroke.

His initial differential diagnosis was, "Well, it's either frontotemporal dementia or early-onset Alzheimer's disease."

That was a shocking revelation to both of us, and it was not what we were expecting at all. We had heard of Alzheimer's disease, of course, but we had no idea at all about what frontotemporal dementia (FTD) was. We left Dr. R.'s office in a stunned state, with disbelief and confusion being our primary reactions. We spent the remainder of the day at home, alternately crying and talking about the morning's events and about what the future might hold. Neither of us really knew anything about either disease, but I was determined to find out as much as I could.

One thing that Dr. R. said that stuck with me, and that we often clung to through those early days, was that we were at the beginning. Whatever the diagnosis, at that time, nothing was different from the day before, and we should continue with our lives until something or someone told us to stop. And that is exactly what we did.

The MRI did not show any signs of physiological disease or abnormality. Dr. R. ordered a PET scan, but our insurance would not cover the cost of several thousand dollars, declaring in their denial (twice), that "the results would not affect the treatment or outcome of the condition." That may well have been true, but it would have given us a more definitive diagnosis with which to go forward. I felt angry and indignant that my husband's health and treatment were being controlled by the insurance company.

Coming from a socialized medical system in the United Kingdom, it was incredible to me that Alan's diagnosis and care would be dictated in that way. Somehow, giving Alan's condition an actual name felt like it would be comforting, as if we could, perhaps, at least deal with a more specific word, instead of just a group of symptoms that had no name. It's amazing how much we all try to exert some kind of control even over the most uncontrollable of situations. Also, without a definitive diagnosis, it was difficult to explain to family and friends exactly what was happening. But I guess insurance companies don't care much about comfort or explanation. Or families or feelings.

Alan insisted that we tell no one, not even our sons. He did not want to worry anyone unnecessarily. I think he was a little embarrassed. People who did not know Alan very well usually never even noticed anything was wrong, and if they did, it usually just sounded like a "slip of the tongue" that we all have occasionally.

Eventually, we called it frontotemporal dementia (FTD), because Alan's symptoms seemed to fit with that description the best. Recently, this title was changed to "frontotemporal degeneration."

In November 2007 Alan attended Dr. M-S's office for his comprehensive neuropsychological evaluation. It was a grueling set of tests designed to compare Alan's abilities in a standardized set of physical and mental tests. It took five hours, and when I went back to collect him, he was drained and deflated. Dr. M-S took us into her office and said that she agreed with Dr. R.'s opinion regarding the differential diagnosis, but that given Alan's relatively young age and symptoms, she was leaning towards frontotemporal dementia. "I'm so sorry, you must be devastated," Dr. M-S said.

Devastated? Well, until that point we weren't, because we didn't really understand that there was anything to be devastated about. But we were devastated. Flabbergasted. Shocked. Stunned. Crushed and any other adjective that could be used to describe our state of disbelief. Following that revelation, I spent a lot of time on the Internet researching FTD and other non-Alzheimer's dementias.

I was devastated, of course. I am very good at putting on a brave face, but I was devastated. I could talk incessantly with a good degree of bravado, but inside I was a quivering wreck. It couldn't be true. Not Thelly! Not my Alan who made a living talking to people. What the heck was FTD anyway?

It became my quest to find out. I read everything I could discover, emailed people at various facilities all over the world who were conducting research studies, and talked to as many people who would listen.

One article, written by Dr. Bob Fay while he was in the early stages of Pick's Disease (a form of FTD), made a particular impression upon me. Dr. Fay presented his article to an international conference in 2003.

I identified some of the things Alan was experiencing with those described by Dr. Fay. One thing that really scared me though was the fact that Dr. Fay, at the time of his writing, had been diagnosed six years earlier in 2003. He was still able to have cognitive thoughts and write about his symptoms.

Six years! The thought of dealing with increasing mental deterioration of my beloved husband for that long, or even longer, was extremely daunting. It filled me with dread. In fact, the average lifespan following diagnosis of FTD is between four and ten years. So perhaps Dr. Fay was either diagnosed very early in his disease, or he was on the high end of the "average" time for some reason. Dr. Fay died in November of 2011 after at least fifteen years of struggling bravely with Pick's disease.

There are so many variants of FTD; it is impossible to always have a specific diagnosis. Many of the symptoms "overlap" or mimic those of other diseases. Also, many FTD patients develop other neurological conditions such as ALS (Lou Gehrig's disease), Parkinson's, or Motor Neuron Disease among others. Whatever the presentation, the outcome is the same: untreatable, incurable, neurological deterioration culminating in death. I spoke with various physicians and psychiatrists, speech therapists and neurological experts at my work, but Alan remained in his "I don't want to know" mode and would just occasionally ask a question about his condition.

We began to look at every little slip of the tongue or typical middle-aged "forgetful" moment very differently. I would frequently reassure him I too went into rooms and forgot what it was I went in them for.

I missed sharing the catastrophe with him. Does that sound odd? It was happening to him, to us. But the one person I would always have shared my fears and misgivings with was not able to listen to them anymore. I do not confide in people very readily, except to Alan. We had the kind of ESP thing many couples have, and we always knew when something needed to be discussed. But not anymore. That was all about to change.

After numerous attempts and periods out of work during that time, Alan finally managed to find a job as an independent contractor with a courier service, using his own vehicle and working from home. They would radio him with a job, and he would go and pick up or drop off whatever and wherever they said. He did a couple of "long-haul" jobs out of town. That scared me to death. Over time, he would call me to MapQuest directions, as he would frequently get lost, even in downtown Phoenix where he had been many times. I would respond respectfully, as always. I never wanted to make him feel like an idiot. He could not read a map ("Forgot my reading glasses."), and he could not read street signs properly either. The job lasted a little under a year and, ultimately, they let him go. Alan declared, "I've had enough. I left."

He stayed at home from March of 2008.

Alan was still very proud, and he would not admit that his problem was so advanced. Of course, being at home gave him the ability to slip to the bar every afternoon to meet with his buddies. I often came home to find him asleep in the chair. He would sometimes be argumentative or belligerent, but I had learned to give him space or leave for a while. He was always repentant afterwards or the next day. He remained loving and engaged in our relationship, bragging to his friends about my success (always exaggerated) at work and about how proud he was of me. You would have thought I was running the whole place the way he spoke. He had been that way throughout our whole relationship. He felt very proud and fortunate.

The boys lived independently, but they were close by and visited regularly. We remained a close-knit group, and we were all very involved in each other's lives. We had gained a new step-grandson, Mason, when our eldest son Chris met Amanda in 2006. We happily added two more people to our family.

In January 2008 Alan's mother, Beryl, died, and Alan had to make the trip back to England alone, as I was unable to go. It was one of the last times he ever went anywhere other than the grocery store alone. I was a little worried about the layover in Newark, but he managed to get there and back unscathed and without any problems (well, none I ever heard about anyway). At the funeral he told several relatives and friends about his diagnosis and informed them, "Eventually, I'll be a blithering idiot."

He was able to describe the tests he had been through and what the diagnosis likely meant for his future.

Alan and David dealt with the grief of their mother's death in the same way as they always handled difficult situations: they went out and got very drunk. Over the next couple of years, Alan tried to drink the same way as he had always done. The symptoms of his dementia were severely exacerbated by alcohol, giving me small insights into what was ahead: unintelligible speech, unsteady gait, and belligerence. All symptoms of alcohol overindulgence, I know, but the symptoms were exaggerated by his increasing dementia. Just a small amount of alcohol had the same effect that would have taken three times as much to achieve a few years ago. I found ways to handle it. Sneaky and conniving but necessary ways.

Over the years I had learned to handle the family trait of "binge drinking." I learned to wait until the next morning to say my piece and not try to argue with someone with no reasoning, because they had a few too many. That knowledge was to be of great advantage to me in the years that followed. During the times in our marriage when he got belligerently drunk (even before the FTD), Alan was always contrite and apologetic the next day. He never tried to hurt our children or me, and he was always very ashamed of his behavior the next morning. I never doubted his love for me, but by God, was he a pain when he drank.

My friend Jane and I, and my sister-in-law, Lydia, were well aware of how to handle our men in drink. It was best to ignore them, do your own thing, and wait for the next day. We had many nights and weekends out as couples when us girls had a much better time. Mainly because the guys started early and finished early. A 7:00 p.m. to 8:00 p.m. bedtime was not unusual. That was when the girls were just getting started!

In June 2008 I was promoted at work to manager of my department. I had hesitated to apply, as the position was Monday through Friday, and I had been working three twelve-hour shifts a week and liked my four days off. However, once we had the diagnosis, my friend JoLynn remarked one day that maybe the promotion was "meant to be," as my time would be more flexible. I now know this was very prophetic on her part, as there would be many times to come when I really needed that flexibility. JoLynn became a great ally and support throughout what was to be the hardest part of my life thus far.

In March of that same year Alan and I had been shopping for new summer clothes for him. I went into the men's dressing room with him (to which he did not object, strangely enough) while he tried on his choices. It was the first time that it was very apparent that he was mentally deteriorating. I had to prompt him to get dressed after he had tried shorts and shirts on. He had become confused over the dressing and undressing and stood there looking at me questioningly. I helped him on with his old shorts, amazed at the fact that he did not think it a little odd. I was shocked and distressed I had started to become such a "parental" figure in our relationship.

In the summer we went to Sedona for a long weekend break to celebrate my promotion at work. Alan could not appreciate the beautiful scenery and was argumentative about where we ate, where we parked, and where we walked. He was so uncomfortable outside his own environment, but I just thought he was being difficult. I was irritated and disappointed.

I steeled myself for what was to come, but no amount of planning could have prepared me for our future. My heart ached for everything that was disappearing right before my eyes:

My life, my love, my partner, my friend.

Eight

MONEY, MONEY, MONEY

*A*fter he was no longer able to work in March of 2008, Alan became a "househusband." He was an excellent homemaker and did everything in our house: cleaning, laundry, shopping, and yard and pool work. The only thing he did not do was cook, but since he never had, apart from very basic, simple things, that wasn't anything new.

I would call him when I was on my way home from work to give instructions on how to put the chicken I had prepared into the oven so that it would be ready when I got there. However, as time went by, the conversations were so long, "Take the dish out of the fridge, turn the oven on to "Bake," turn it up to 400 degrees," etc., that I gave up calling with instructions because he could not follow even the simplest direction. Adam and I would almost be home by the time I got him to understand. It was not easy to keep the conversation respectful when communication was so difficult and frustrating.

At that time Adam and I were carpooling, as he worked close to me. He would listen to those conversations with disbelief. He was just beginning to understand what was happening to his dad. Along with his brother, Chris, he was a little in denial at the time about the severity of his dad's increasing disability. I am sure it was very difficult for them to comprehend what was happening, and it was just as hard for me to explain. Because Alan appeared "normal" in most respects, it was almost impossible to convey the seriousness of his prognosis. I felt so alone at that time. No one seemed to understand what was beginning to happen. I tried to tell people, but I never seemed to be able to get it across to them. Maybe I was understating it, because I didn't want to believe it myself.

In August of 2008 our third grandson, Zane Alexander, was born to Chris and his fiancée Amanda. Alan was delighted and loved to spend time with the new baby, just so long as I was not spending what he perceived as too much time away from his needs. He loved being with Zane as he could make baby noises and not have to actually talk to him using real words, which was becoming increasingly difficult for Alan.

In the twelve months since his diagnosis, Alan had gone from being an independent, capable adult to a much more passive partner in respect to decision making and his ability to function out in the world. His world became our house, the local store, and his favorite bar where he had his comfort zones. Even those familiar places were not always havens for him. His deteriorating speech made social occasions increasingly difficult. Even buying groceries was a major exercise in patience and tolerance for all concerned.

Later that same year, Alan returned for a follow-up assessment by Dr. M-S at the Neurological Institute. Although he did not relish the thought of another five-hour ordeal, Alan did the testing. The doctor reported there had been a significant deterioration since the last assessment the year before.

When the time was up for completing all the exercises, Alan said that he did not finish some of them, because he was "bored and didn't want to." In truth, he could not complete the tests or follow the instructions. When we sat down to talk afterwards, Dr. M-S reiterated that FTD was still the most likely diagnosis, and so that was what we continued to call it. She asked that Alan come back again in a year for further assessment. He reluctantly agreed, but once outside, he told me he would not go back. I am sure that he said that because he was embarrassed and felt inadequate. Alan was still adamant he did not wish to be told what was likely to happen in the near and more distant future. But as his wife and as a nurse, I felt more comfortable being armed with as much information as I could get.

I researched voraciously, seeking out information from various sources, talking with neurologists and psychiatrists at my work, reading papers and articles, and associating myself with various support groups. I still could not really believe it. I didn't want to. Surely this could not be happening to us. How corny! Everyone thinks bad things never happen to "people like us." But they do. All the time.

It's like being in the middle of a tornado, with everything swirling around you. Nothing is under control. I hate that.

Alan's neurologist, Dr. R. declared around that time, "Since there is no treatment I can offer, you may as well go and be followed by your family doctor now. Maybe you should try Aricept."

Aricept is a medication commonly used for slowing down the symptoms of Alzheimer's disease. Dr. R. also stated there was little evidence that Aricept or any other medication for Alzheimer's had been shown to be effective in FTD. Our family doctor, Dr. A., although not knowledgeable about FTD at all, was very open to the explanations and to the articles and research that I provided for her. She proved to be a good, if infrequent, resource over the months and years to come. Alan was so physically healthy, fit, and strong that he almost never went to the doctor's office, except for routine physicals and so on.

Following up on some research I had done online, Alan agreed to participate in a research study at University Medical Center in Tucson, Arizona. We developed a great relationship with Maya, a fellow at the university, who was conducting research for her PhD. Maya was working with Professor B., who is a world-renowned authority on FTD. Professor B.'s particular focus is on primary progressive aphasia (PPA), a variant of FTD. Alan was demonstrating many of the symptoms of PPA. Word finding, verbal memory problems, and difficulty with learning and comprehension are classic in the variant.

Memory issues are not usually prevalent in the early to middle stages of PPA, and Alan was not exhibiting any symptoms of memory loss other than memory for words. Maya came to our house to conduct some tests and videotape interviews. Alan really enjoyed the attention and hammed it up for the camera in true "Thelly" style! As a follow-up, we travelled to Tucson at a later date for a functional MRI and more verbal testing. Alan tolerated the whole process very well. He was able to explain that he wanted to do it because, even if it would not help him, the research could eventually help someone else.

It was about that time that I started to "interpret" for him. He would look to me whenever anyone asked a question. Like a child to his mother. And that was how it had become. It was a weird parent-child relationship with my husband of over thirty years.

Early in 2009 Alan began to hint he should be paid for doing the housework. He had come to realize having no income of his own was beginning to restrict his freedom somewhat. Thus began a period of great discord and unrest in our house. Since I paid all the bills electronically, and he had a debit card with which to pay for groceries (he was still shopping at that time), we hardly ever used cash. But that led to many confrontations, and Alan's new stock phrases became "Got nothing!" and "Not a man!"

He associated his lack of money with a slight to his manhood and expressed that to me many times. To Alan, like many men, money represented power and control and having no tangible cash meant he had neither of those things. We worked out a plan in which I would give him cash each week in return for the chores he did. At first he thought that $75 a week was fair, but when I explained that it added up to $300 a month, like another car payment in fact, he agreed to $25 every Friday.

He was still going to the bar several times a week to meet up with his friends. For a little while, he would save his money by not going out and then use it all at once, but that didn't last long. He could not grasp the fact that once it was gone, it was gone, and he had to wait until the next "payday" for more. He started to accuse me of not giving him any money at all. He denied I had given it to him, even if I wrote it down and showed him the list.

He was beginning to become very suspicious and paranoid. Sometimes it would get to the point where I would tearfully ask, "Do you really think I would try to cheat you? I love you!"

His face would dissolve into sadness, as he sheepishly whispered, "No."

At that time, he went through so much money that I started to believe he was either losing it, or someone was taking advantage of him by not giving him change or charging him too much for his drinks. I started looking through drawers and cupboards, all the obvious places at first.

Later, I found some other hiding places: inside pockets and socks, tucked away underneath things in his nightstand, and even under his nightstand. He also lost his driver's license twice, two sets of house keys, his wedding ring, debit card (which someone found and used fraudulently), and so much money I lost count. I cancelled his bank cards and suffered his wrath when he would call me at work, screaming abuse because the (old, expired) card I had given him as a replacement would not work.

The clerks at Walgreens were very understanding and helpful; they would talk to me on the phone and then give him whatever it was he was trying to buy (deodorant, shaving foam, whatever), and I would stop by on my way home to pay for it.

For quite some time, there was a hiatus in Alan's behavior. The changes were so subtle, so insidious, that the deterioration was difficult to detect, especially to me, seeing him every day. Other people noticed changes more easily as they did not see him every day. We took each setback with dignity as Alan's capabilities were slowly eroded. But by May of 2009 Alan was experiencing more significant physical symptoms.

Some of them were attributed as side effects from medications we were trying out to help alleviate other symptoms. Hot flashes, depression, tingling sensations in his head, hands, and feet, sudden jerks of the legs almost like a startle reflex. The list went on and on. As is common with most non-Alzheimer's dementias, Alan was prescribed many of the drugs commonly tried with Alzheimer's patients, including Aricept and the Exelon Patch. Both had horrible side effects and made him feel much worse. The intent of these drugs is to slow down the progression of the disease, but there is currently no evidence they are effective in this way, and I certainly did not notice any difference in Alan's condition or symptoms.

Of course, in the words of Alexander Pope, "Hope springs eternal in the human breast."

I often agreed to try things even though I knew it was fruitless. It's hard to explain. My soul would not give up on him. I figured that if it didn't hurt, we would try it. I gradually stopped giving him each one as it became increasingly obvious nothing could save my dwindling, once-bright, stargazing partner now.

Nine

MISSING IN ACTION

In March of 2009 I wrote in my journal:

"I miss having someone to talk with. Those times are getting fewer and farther between, although Alan does not seem to notice. For him, life is just the same, and I often wonder if I am imagining his lessening awareness of me and my needs, or if I am just being selfish?"

The long silences were like black holes in our home. I slowly learned to be patient, to capitulate more, and, for the sake of peace, to keep my mouth shut. It was a lonely time.

Reasoning and rationalizing became things of the past. Alan was still seeking solace in drink, and he was clinging more to the idea of friends rather than the actual friends themselves. It was as if having friends and people around him reinforced that he was still part of the real world, and everything was okay.

It was about that time that I joined the FTD caregiver support group at the local Banner Alzheimer's Institute. I had attended a lecture given by Dr. G. (Maribeth) at my work. Because I identified with so many of the things she talked about, I approached her after the lecture to discuss his symptoms. She was so kind as she listened and empathized. After only a few sentences, I broke down. That was really the first time I had met someone who actually seemed to understand what was happening to us. She emailed me afterwards with the details of the next group meeting, and I went along with some trepidation. Support groups were something I recommended to my patients and their families weren't they? They were not something I thought I would ever attend. They were just not *me* really.

Anyway, there I was in a small library at the Alzheimer's Institute with three or four other nervous-looking women, all of whom introduced herself as the caregiver of a spouse with FTD. I was actually quite shocked that so many people were talking about the same things that were happening in my life. I found out later it was only the second meeting of the group. As of 2013, the group has more than fifty members, all of whom are caregivers, wives, husbands, adult children, or friends of someone who has FTD. And that's just in Phoenix. There is an epidemic it seems.

The group was led by Geri, a doctor of nursing practice working with the neurologists at the Alzheimer's Institute, and Rebekah, a social worker from a local hospice organization. They had a wonderful understanding of the trials faced by caregivers of this horrible disease and were patient, kind, and knowledgeable.

I spent the first two sessions in tears as I described the pain of the previous two years. The other members kindly sympathized and listened. I could barely speak as I described the disappearance of my beloved husband. Each month, as we went around the table so that we could all introduce ourselves and briefly describe our situations, there were many tears shed. But we learned a lot and found it comforting to identify with the problems we each faced on a daily basis.

Sometimes I would pass when it was my turn because I was unable to speak.

One thing that was particularly noticeable was the young age of almost all the patients. One member's husband was only forty-eight. Alan was fifty-three at that time. I never shared with Alan that I was attending the support group but would take the afternoon off from my work to attend (So JoLynn was right about the flexibility after all). I remember feeling quite envious of the members' spouses who were able to attend the institute as a patient. The neurologist, Dr. Y., sounded so engaged and energetic about helping his patients, I really thought Alan would benefit from seeing him, but our insurance at the time prevented that. Later, when the insurance provider changed, Alan was able to see Dr. Y. and get the long-awaited PET scan, which would finally give us more information about the progression of his disease.

By then Alan seemed to be sinking deeper into depression. He stated that he didn't "feel like a man" anymore. I tried to distract him with jigsaw puzzles and DVDs but that only worked for a little while. He could not even work the DVD player by himself. Sometimes Alan would call either Adam or me, because he could not get the TV to work. Phone conversations were extremely difficult and one-sided. It was like a game of "twenty questions." Eventually we would arrive at what we thought was the correct problem that needed to be solved.

One day, while attending an important work function, I had to call Amanda to go and turn the TV on for Alan, as he could not manage it. He spent a lot of time watching TV but could only watch reruns of shows with which he was familiar, so he did not have to follow a new story. (By the way, if anyone needs prompting on the scripts of *Two and a Half Men* or *Ghost Whisperer*, I'm your gal.). He was still doing all the housework and slipping off to the bar in the afternoons to see his friends, most of whom were not there but at work. He would just buy a drink and sit in the bar, not really communicating with anyone, but apparently feeling like he was part of the real world.

On the weekends when I was home, things were mostly okay, just the occasional bickering, which we'd been doing for thirty-five years, so nothing new there then. Sometimes, however, there were meltdowns, which usually ended up with both of us in tears. Alan would cry, because he was scared of his extremes of emotion, and I would cry mostly because, well—to be honest—I was scared too. But I was also angry and resentful that the man I had shared my life with and had been a friend and partner to for over thirty-five years had an actual excuse to be mean to me! I begged him to "fight" it, which I knew was impossible, but I so dearly wanted my Alan back. We would sit on the bed or the floor in our room and hug each other, sobbing in our shared raw pain.

Isolation, desolation, and despair.

Neither of us could even begin to understand what it was like for the other. We had always shared everything. So it was doubly painful. He had no clue of the level of support I needed. I could not even begin to understand what it felt like for him.

In his increasingly rare, lucid moments, I would try to explain to him how frustrating it was to try to reason with someone who had no insight into his unreasonableness. Alan shared that he sometimes had "terrible thoughts" when he was alone during the day. He felt useless and alone and a huge burden. It scared me he would think of harming himself in some way, but I understood it too.

Dr. A., our family doctor, prescribed an antidepressant around that time, and it helped a lot. I asked the boys to check in on Alan more often when I was at work, and I put aside my own fears and anger to take better care of the man I loved.

One Saturday we were being couch potatoes and watching yet another rerun (a favorite Western movie, *She Wore a Yellow Ribbon*). Alan suddenly stood up and said more words in one sentence than he had said in a long time. He was very worried he hadn't paid his bills or taxes, and they would be "coming for me." I reassured him all the bills were paid, and I had taken care of the taxes, so not to worry. It was as if he had been sleeping for three years and just woke up. It was strange and surreal. And it was sad, so sad. It was the first sign of the paranoia that was to follow.

That was one of the last times Alan gave any indication of understanding the real world.

Alan's speech continued to deteriorate, although cursing and abuse came readily to his lips. By May of 2010 it had become more halting and difficult for others to understand. He would always try to tell people or have me explain that he had a "speech problem."

I always knew Alan loved me. Those spontaneous kisses and hugs, just a little touch when we passed by each other, had been some of our favorite things. But that feeling of my being cherished was beginning to disappear. Alan was unable to look beyond his own needs and appreciate the pain or distress of others. That even extended to laughing; his once-prevalent sense of humor had all but disappeared too. Or it would appear inappropriately in social situations. He would sometimes use a nervous laugh in an attempt to cover the fact that he could not say a word or phrase, but not as an appropriate response to something funny.

We did, however, continue to dance around the kitchen randomly to music on the TV or play our old albums on the record player. His love of dancing never left him right up until the end of his life. We would laugh together at our uncoordinated skipping and twirling. At least there was still something in which we could still find a little fun.

I so missed all the little things couples have between them. Like those little secrets only the two of you know. I missed laughing at stupid stuff. I missed the specialness of our relationship.

One of our favorite sayings was "I love you one more than you love me." The joke being that whatever you said in return, the first person's love was "one more" and could not be surpassed. Everyone has those private jokes and ways of saying and doing things, some of which go back to the early days of their relationships. There are also those very private tragedies that happen to so many people but are rarely discussed except between the two of you. Lying like spoons in your bed and whispering in the dark so you don't wake the kids, or your in-laws, or guests. I missed those times. I miss them still and always will.

Once, when we were first married and on vacation, Alan and I pretended we didn't know one another and loudly picked one another up in the bar of a hotel. We got some very strange and disapproving looks from people (It was 1977 after all.), and we laughed all the way back to our hotel.

Before his illness began, whenever I was sick with a cold or something, Alan would let me sleep, bring me tea and toast, and constantly check on me to see if I needed medicine, water, or Kleenex. When the boys were small, he would take care of them so that I could study. We loved to "people-watch," make inappropriate remarks about almost everything, and laugh at silly, childish jokes that did not mean anything to anyone else.

Christmas was always a big deal. Alan would buy me a new outfit, a pair of boots, jewelry, and perfume. He always surprised me with his choices, which were very good and just what I would have chosen for myself. He would secretly shop for them, wrap them, and place them under the tree. But he couldn't help pointing them out and telling me not to peek. I never did, but he got a kick out of being all secretive and conspiratorial.

On Saturday nights, we would watch our favorite British comedies on PBS, even though we had seen them many times before. We would enjoy the shared connection with our roots and the familiar English countryside scenery in *Last of the Summer Wine*. I cannot bring myself to watch them now.

All of it slowly disappeared like a beautiful ice sculpture at a wedding, melting insidiously until only a mere puddle was left.

In our case, it was a puddle of love.

Ten

TRAVEL TROUBLES

*E*arly in 2010, like many spouses who are caregivers for terminally ill people, I decided to plan one last big trip. I knew that Alan's deterioration meant that a trip would not be possible for much longer, and I wanted to try, at least, to make some good lasting memories.

I was being realistic about the timeline. I knew it would not be long before we could no longer do any of those fun, middle-aged things. I knew the trip would be difficult. Alan's behavior was often akin to that of a petulant five-year-old. I didn't care. I was determined that he should have as a good a time as I could make for him, for both of us.

We decided to go and visit a very good friend, Steve, with whom Alan had worked on QE2. They shared a cabin for several years and became very close on their travels around the world. We had always kept in touch over the years. Steve now lives aboard a catamaran off Tortola in the British Virgin Islands. So in May of 2010 we set off on our journey to the Caribbean.

The journey was long and tiring. It was like travelling with a bratty child. Alan refused to carry anything, he kept trying to wander off, and he threw tantrums everywhere: at the airport, on the plane, and anytime we had to wait for more than a few minutes for anything. But two plane trips, a ferryboat ride, and a taxi later, we arrived on Tortola. Steve picked us up and took us to the cottage we had rented, and we settled in for our vacation.

Alan's obsessive compulsion to try to control his environment extended to arranging and rearranging his clothing, pacing around the cottage, and making the bed over and over again. He was, however, very pleasant with the owners of the property who lived next door. I could not make him understand that he could not just go off exploring on his own. Our fight ended with me responding to his question "Why?" with a yell of "BECAUSE YOU HAVE DEMENTIA!"

I was so frustrated, exhausted, and stressed by both the journey and our new surroundings, which I had not realized would be so anxiety-inducing for both of us.

Once again throughout the trip, the money issue came up. Even though we had been to the bank before we left Phoenix and withdrawn *his* spending money, Alan felt the need to top that up by visiting the ATM a couple of times during the trip. It made me laugh though, because he never actually spent any of the money. It never occurred to him to pay a check or bar bill. He just needed to have it in his pocket. If I ever asked him to pay for something, he would look at me in disgust, and then reluctantly hand over as little as possible, or say he did not have it with him. It was funny, because being cheap had never been one of his faults.

All things considered, it was a good time. Steve made us very welcome, showing us around the island and taking us on many trips on his boat, Aristocat, to snorkel and to visit the surrounding islands. There was constant sunshine, tropical temperatures, and the scenery was stunning. Beautiful white, sandy beaches, lush rainforest, and a warm, blue ocean filled with marine life. A dream come true.

I was hoping for a relaxing break, but my wish was only partly fulfilled. I felt like Alan's mother rather than his wife. His behavior was so childlike. I was disappointed by the fact that he did not seem to appreciate the beauty of our surroundings. He mostly stayed on the boat when I was snorkeling or swimming, only venturing into the water once or twice, and then staying very close to the boat. He was afraid to swim, which saddened me. He had always been such a strong, athletic swimmer and loved the water.

Perhaps I had put off the "big trip" for too long?

There were a couple of incidents when Alan completely misread situations and dragged me away from conversations with people he didn't know. He couldn't understand why I was walking around half-dressed. He kept making eye-rolling gestures about the impropriety of how I was dressed (in a bathing suit on the boat).

"SAILING IN THE CARIBBEAN, MAY 2010"

Steve was saddened and surprised by Alan's deterioration, but I had pre-warned him about what was happening, and he handled everything very well. We spent the evening hours on Steve's boat or going to local restaurants that Steve knew, and reminiscing about the old days. Steve and Alan (well, mostly Steve) recalled places they had been, other crew members on the ship, and scrapes they had got into and out of.

The journey home was equally as frustrating as the journey to Tortola. One of the things a wife doesn't usually have to think about is letting her husband go into the men's restroom alone. I didn't feel comfortable leaving him while I went into the women's restroom at the airport, as I was worried he would come out of the men's room before me, wander off, and get lost. So I waited until we got on the plane. Alan threw a couple of tantrums at the airport and ran over the same woman's foot three times with the carry-on he had so graciously agreed to pull along on our trip home. I silently mouthed an apology and that he had dementia to her. She smiled kindly and said it was okay.

I have to admit, I was sometimes embarrassed by Alan's behavior since he looked so normal and healthy and relatively young to be so cognitively impaired. As time went by though, I became more immune to those feelings, and I decided that if people didn't like it, it was just too bad! As long as no one was hurt, it didn't really matter. I would apologize and move on.

The realization of what was going to happen in Alan's future prompted Steve to come out to Phoenix in August of that year, and we spent lots of time just hanging out in the back yard, swimming in the pool, and eating and drinking. It was a relaxing time. Alan enjoyed the sense of normality that Steve's visit brought him. In his own environment, he was more relaxed, less anxious. He swam and sat with us sometimes, but once the conversation became a little too much, he would retreat into the house. We reminisced about old times and old friends from the 1970s when we all first met. We went to a preseason football game and showed Steve some of our local Phoenix sights.

The only issue that came up was when Steve expressed he wanted to visit the Grand Canyon while he was in Arizona. To drive there and back from Phoenix in one day is a long trip, five hours in each direction, so we were discussing Steve and me sharing the driving. Alan was adamant he would drive some of the way, which was not an option at that time, so we did not go.

Steve never did get to see the Grand Canyon.

Driving and dementia could be a whole chapter in and of itself.

As with many FTD and other dementia patients, driving became a huge issue. Driving represents independence and control. The loss of this power is devastating to the dementia sufferer, and the prospect of them driving is equally scary to their loved ones. Alan had no insight into his loss of judgment or ability to make good decisions, both of which are, of course, vital for safe driving. I had noticed his coordination and decision making while driving had become very erratic. But he was extremely defensive and saw any discussion as criticism, something he had never handled well. He would swing out to the right when making a left turn, cutting into the next lane. He would never know which direction to go, even in our own neighborhood, and made sudden and dramatic changes in speed and direction while moving too fast. I always made a point of saying, "I'll drive, if you like," and gradually, more often than not, he began to acquiesce. But there was quite a while there when it was a battle to have him be the passenger. Another little piece of independence eroded.

I loaned one of our cars to our son Adam, and I was at work all day in the other one, so that left little opportunity for Alan to drive anyway. If he wanted to see his friends at the bar, either he would walk, or I would drop him off and pick him up. Alan had no idea about his lack of judgment, and I was very concerned about our liability in the event of an accident.

I enlisted the help of our family physician, Dr. A. Better for her to be the bad guy than me. Alan liked her a lot. She had proven to be a good ally in the past, and she had always treated Alan with dignity and respect. We went along to her office for a routine physical. At the end of the visit, she said to Alan, "I want to talk to you about driving."

I had called her ahead of time and explained the situation. She agreed it was time for "the talk." She agreed to be the one to tell him so that I would not be the one taking something else away from Alan. She gently explained to him if he were to have an accident while driving, because of his dementia diagnosis, both she and I would be liable, because we knew about his illness, and we had allowed him to drive anyway. She mentioned she is duty bound to inform the Department of Motor Vehicles to which Alan replied he would happily go and take a test. (Many FTD patients take the test and pass with flying colors, by the way).

Since he had little to no insight into his disabilities, Alan took the conversation as a personal insult and thought us ridiculous. After Dr. A. had finished talking, Alan threw what could only be described as a tantrum and walked out of her office, declaring that it was a conspiracy and that I had to control everything. It was expressed as, "You, you did!" And, of course, I had. That reaction continued for several weeks afterwards, with Alan asking Adam frequently to take him to the DMV. Interestingly, he never tried to drive down there himself. Adam would agree to take him and say "Tomorrow," and then Alan would finally give up asking. The next day he would not remember he had asked Adam already. One has to take advantage of the forgetfulness in those situations.

The theme pervaded throughout the rest of the summer and into the fall when his sisters came to visit from England.

The day after the doctor's visit Alan walked to the bar while I was at work and got very drunk. I came home to find him stumbling around the house in his underwear. When I asked him to come and sit down, he wandered out into the street and walked for about ten minutes around our neighborhood, still only in his underwear. I followed him at a distance until he returned home. In spite of his behavior, I do believe on some level, he knew he was deteriorating and would have to accept the rules that were being imposed upon him. Clearly and understandably, he did not like that.

In September 2010 Alan's sisters Susan and Lorraine, came to visit. They had all had a very close relationship in their younger years. Alan was the baby of the family for nine years before David came along, so having two older sisters with only two years between each of them meant they spent lots of time together as children. The three of them had many happy hours playing, and they have some wonderful memories. Susan is a nurse too, and I had been explaining for a long time about Alan's condition, which she understood very well. Lorraine, on the other hand, was quite shocked at how much Alan had deteriorated in the two-and-a-half years since she had last seen him at their mother's funeral in 2008. They were both surprised and sympathetic at what I was dealing with every day.

Whenever we spent time out by the pool sunning ourselves and chatting, Alan would come and sit with us for a few minutes, and then he would petulantly go inside. He really struggled with the fact that he could not join in the conversation. Of course, we would try to include him as much as possible, but the truth was he was no longer capable of that much social interaction. In a phone conversation with Lorraine's husband, Glenn, Alan announced loudly, "She thinks she rules the fucking world!" He meant me, of course. It was one of the longest sentences Alan had spoken at a time when he could often barely string more than two or three words together.

59

"SISTERS VISIT, SEPTEMBER 2010"

During meals out in restaurants, he would usually sit quietly and eat his food, always allowing me to order for him and communicate his needs to the wait staff. His awkwardness in talking to strangers eroded his confidence significantly. He did demonstrate some adolescent behavior while out with his sisters, and they were able to smooth things over with the poor innocent bystander and get Alan back on track. He had no tolerance for what we would consider minor irritations, such as someone tapping on the back of our booth seat for example. He would respond by swatting at the man when he walked by to go to the bathroom. Susan and Lorraine made apologies and explanations and all was well.

Alan's social filters seemed to be fading away at a rapid rate. He would point at people for an extended length of time, make garbled comments in a loud voice, and so on. At that time it was like living with an immature ten-year-old. If you have ever watched the character Sofia in the TV sitcom *The Golden Girls*, you will know exactly what I am talking about. An outing to the supermarket became a minefield of redirection, apologies, and explanations. Sometimes Alan would push the cart, at other times he would refuse. There was very little consistency. At least life was never boring.

On the last weekend of Susan and Lorraine's visit, David and Lydia came over from Los Angeles so we could all spend David's birthday together. Of course that meant that we had a very full house, plus Adam, Pamela, and Jack came over too. Alan handled it reasonably well. We spent a lot of time at home so he would have the freedom to come in and out of the group without us all being in a public place where he would be more uncomfortable. We made a lot of concessions to his needs, and it was mostly a good time. One night he did not want to sleep with me, so he and David slept together (not for the first time) in our bed. I was so grateful that the whole family was so willing to do whatever it took to make Alan comfortable.

We went out to breakfast and dinner a few times, but it was obvious Alan could not handle the social situations of our large family group. He did not act out but sat quietly at the table, waiting for the food I had ordered for him ("You know."), and then silently eating it. Once again, he was a spectator on the sidelines, watching our family fun. It was an outward expression of family fun from all of us. But it was masking the great sadness each one of us harbored. Dad, brother, and husband. None of those roles were significant to Alan then. I think he still knew we were important to him but not specifics like names or roles.

Susan and Lorraine left with David and Lydia to spend the last few days of their trip with them in Los Angeles. After all the guests had gone, Alan continued some of the habits he had developed while we had a house full of people. For example, when we had four extra people in the house, the dishwasher was full every day. After we went back to it being just him and me, he continued to turn it on every evening, even if there were only five or six pieces in there.

His obsessions with clothes and arranging and rearranging his dresser drawers and closet got much worse. He had developed the habit of changing his clothes at least five or six times a day, throwing the discarded ones in the laundry, and running the washing machine at least once a day, sometimes more. We went through a lot of T-shirts.

One day I went to pick Alan up from the bar (it was a hard habit to break). He tried to use a key from the lock for his bike, which was at home, on another bike in the parking lot, insisting that it was his. As always, he took some persuading to convince him that it was not his bike. There were several occasions described in my journal at that time when I expressed my frustration at not being able to understand Alan as he tried to explain something to me. Those episodes usually ended up with both of us in tears. Often it would be about the TV remote, for example. Alan could not always get it to turn on the TV, change channels, or something else that he wanted to do.

It was so very hard not to feed into his frustration, and it was painful to watch as he was chipped away by the insidious thing that was eating away at his brain. I often wanted to scream, "Who are you and what have you done with my husband?"

Like a scene from *The Invisible Man*, my darling Alan seemed to be disappearing before my eyes. Although my deep love for him never waned, I often felt myself wanting to withdraw from the relationship emotionally, as if to protect myself from the pain of losing him. But I couldn't. I couldn't and wouldn't abandon him and our love.

I wrote in my journal: "My grief gets worse every day."

Alan would often call me during that time while I was at work and scream unintelligible abuse. I rarely knew what it was about. One time it was about "coins in a bag" (Money again!).

Adam went over to see what the problem was, and he could not understand either. They sat down to watch a soccer game, but Alan could not get over his lost coins and stormed out of the room to continue looking. He was slamming doors and drawers, throwing things around, breaking the trash can. Adam drove him to a few places to look for the bag with no success. Then, when they got back, Adam called the hairdresser where Alan had been that morning, and lo and behold, he had left a ziplock bag with coins in it there. What was more surprising was that before Adam came over, Alan had remembered the location of the hairdresser's salon, walked there, managed to explain what he wanted done to his hair, and paid them. Even though he left his bag of coins, just organizing that trip by himself was amazing. Another example of how FTD does not travel in a straight line.

Adam took him back there, and they retrieved the bag. After that he settled down, but those times when he was like a dog with a bone over something, it was pretty unbearable.

I had noticed in November of 2009 that even though I was giving him cash (at one point, $220 in less than three weeks), Alan was still using his bank debit card sometimes. When I asked him about it, he said he had used it for groceries or at Walgreens, but at that time, he was no longer doing the shopping as he did not drive. By the way, when I describe our "conversations" at that time, I mean we eventually got around to the actual topic by playing charades until I understood what he meant. I often looked for his stash of cash at that point but never found it.

I began to see Alan as very much a Jekyll-and-Hyde character, never knowing from one day, or even one hour, to the next who would be present. He would occasionally refer to "the thing...my head" or just point to his head. When in a social group, he would either have me explain, or he would point to his mouth and somehow demonstrate that he had a speech problem. He never understood how deeply I was affected by the terrible turn in our lives. It was like living on a knife-edge. I tried to remember happier times and used the memories to get me through the dark days.

At that time, we were still occasionally able to reminisce together and to laugh and smile about old friends and times. We pored over old photographs and videos. Alan was looking out at the world as if he was behind a window through which he could not pass. Locked in his own world, he desperately clung to those familiar things he could remember and with which he still felt comfortable.

We could still often be seen waltzing and jiving around our kitchen island like a couple of teenagers when a favorite old song came on the TV or radio.

Then the music changed again.

We had to alter our tempo.

Eleven

OBSESSIONS

By the end of 2010 Alan's speech and comprehension were much worse. Conversations were almost impossible for the most part, although occasionally the old Alan would pop out to say hello. He was sleeping a lot during the day and almost all of every evening after dinner. In addition, he would still sleep for eight to ten hours a night. I decided to broach the question of day care again, even though Alan had been very much against it in the past. I even presented it as voluntary work, but he said, "Not nothing," meaning he would not work for free. I decided to leave it for a few weeks and then bring it up again. Sometimes he would say "Yes," and then the next time "No."

We had completed wills, power of attorney paperwork, and advance directives back in 2009. Two years into his illness Alan had fully accepted there would come a time when he could no longer make decisions for himself. He had always been very clear about his wishes even before he ever knew he was sick. We had talked many times about various scenarios over the years, and he signed the paperwork gladly. He resolutely believed life should not be prolonged without quality, and when you're dead, you're dead.

I was beginning to realize it was best not to give him a choice, just a decision and then deal with the fallout afterwards. That proved to be a good tactic to learn, because in the coming months, I was to make many decisions that did not include Alan. Eventually he either accepted that I would always do what was right or forgot he was against it in the first place. Presenting a decision again later when he had forgotten the initial conversation worked well.

Cleaning and housework in general had become totally obsessive by then, to the point where I felt like I was intruding in my own house. Alan would complain if I moved anything or left anything out of place. In my more frustrated moments I would yell, "I live here too you know!"

What had changed then, however, was the quality of the housework was very different. He put dirty dishes back in the cupboard (because he would empty the dishwasher before it had been turned on), silverware in the wrong places, nonfood items in the refrigerator, and dirty clothes in the closet. Alan expected a great deal of praise for his efforts in the house, and he would be sulky and petulant when the praise wasn't forthcoming. He seemed so plausible at times, and I felt horrible that I was so unfeeling. I was living with a sulky preteen who did not appreciate anything at all.

The frequent clothes changing continued. The washing machine and dryer were on almost constantly. He was so proud he was doing productive work in the house; I never had the heart to discourage him. The constant rearranging of clothes and opening and closing of drawers meant that getting dressed took a very long time, but I was determined to enable Alan's independence with his own care for as long as possible. I tried not to interfere, wanting to let him make his own choices.

Losing control is difficult for all of us. I wanted to prolong Alan's sense of control as much as possible. His personal hygiene, which is often one of the first things to go in FTD, was still good though, thankfully. That became obsessive too, as Alan showered several times a day, for example. My mantra was, "If what he is doing does not hurt him or anyone else then why shouldn't he do it?" And so I let him do whatever he wanted using that principle. My love for him would not allow me to make anything more difficult for him than it already was.

One of the newer things that started was an obsession with the air conditioning. Even when it was sixty-five degrees outside, Alan would always have the AC on when I got home from work. He seemed to have increased sensitivity to heat and cold, and he was always looking for a solution to his discomfort. He did not realize that the AC was on and wondered why he was so cold. He would put on extra sweaters and socks to keep warm. But then when he warmed up, instead of taking them off, he cranked up the AC! It was the cause of much agitation and disturbance. Rather than risk a confrontation, I would put on a sweater, take it off, put a throw over my legs, and then take it off. I did whatever it took to deal with the inconsistent temperature. At night I would wait until he had gone to bed and then get up and turn the air off.

There were additional symptoms worsening too. Since early on in his illness Alan had been making what I can only describe as grunting or humming noises when sitting quietly or watching TV. The noise was a little like the sound someone makes when they are agreeing with you during a conversation or tasting something particularly nice: "hm." But it would be totally out of place and completely random. Other people in the family noticed it too and finally began to believe something serious was going on with Alan. When it first started it would be after he had been drinking and then during eating. Then it developed to the point where it was almost constant. I learned from the support group at the Alzheimer's Institute that the humming was a form of comfort for dementia patients, a reassurance for their "inner voice."

By then Adam was noticing big changes with his dad. Having witnessed some of the newer behaviors, he agreed things were getting worse. Adam was, and remains, wonderfully patient and kind. He is a great support for me, often to the detriment of his own feelings. It saddened Adam that Alan lacked the ability to share the things they once had, like watching football together; enjoying the good-natured banter, and commenting on the games.

Chris, Amanda, and their children had moved up to Washington State to be closer to her family. Adam and I spent many hours accommodating Alan's wishes and needs so that his life was as simple as possible. We enabled any behavior that was not dangerous or too disruptive. Of course, over time that became very tiring for both of us. I was beginning to suffer a little from caregiver's fatigue, which Adam recognized. His support grew, and he was very understanding and matter-of-fact about the situation. Nothing was too much trouble for him.

Looking back, I feel badly I did not truly understand how much Adam was hurting at the time. Maybe I could have helped him cope more, but I was so wrapped up in my own pain and Alan's day-to-day care, I could not. I resolved to take much better care of myself moving forward in order to find some peace within myself and to help Alan through that terrible time. Alan's short periods of lucidity often fooled me into thinking maybe we were all wrong, that his condition was not really as bad as we had thought, and he would get well. But deep down in my heart, I knew it was just another form of denial on my part.

The human spirit clings onto the very slightest glimmer of hope, real or imagined. In that place named Denial, you can't forget to stop and enjoy even the smallest victories or moments of joy. Appreciating one incident of acquiescence or a smile or a spontaneous kiss, or just no argument about a request, is a cause for celebration.

Alan's drinking had somewhat reduced by that time, and the references to driving became less frequent, although he still occasionally threatened to go to the DMV and get tested. By Thanksgiving 2010 he was saying in his way that if he had to sit in the house all day, he may as well go back to England. He had, of course, no rational response to questions about what he would do there and where he would live, just that he wanted to go. Perhaps he thought he wouldn't be sick there. Who knows? Alan remained affectionate, kissing and hugging me as he always had. He would still occasionally hint at sex. One day I told him it would be like making love with a stranger, as I didn't know him anymore. He saw that as another reason to leave. It seems even the afflicted mind has pride, resentment, and feelings of rejection.

Looking back at that description in my journal now, I feel very guilty about some of the things I said, but I was in pain and grieving for the man I had lost and sometimes just had to lash out. Of course, Alan did not say those things as clearly as I have written them here, I just inferred from the garbled words and incomplete sentences. At that time he probably understood about one third of what was said to him.

The adolescent behaviors escalated. Alan would sulk, huff, and puff when doing the dishes, for example. He would complain about how many pots and pans there were for, "Two people," even when I offered to do the dishes. He took to storming off when frustrated or slamming dishes around the kitchen. Then he would come back into the room and continuing as if nothing had happened.

Those episodes were little glimpses into what was to come. A peek behind the curtain that was concealing the FTD Wizard.

The money issue came to a head one day when I jokingly asked him about his stash of cash, as he had been going through cash so rapidly. I should point out that Alan's sense of humor was so severely depleted by then I should have known better than to make a joke about such a sensitive subject. He put his face right up to mine and screamed at me, as I had never heard him scream before. It was almost animal-like in its nature, using profanity (which I had heard before, of course, but not with such venom). It was the forerunner of many more episodes to come. That night I wrote in my journal about trying to be serene and not feeding into the madness and anger.

That same day we received the news that Chris and Amanda were expecting a baby girl. At last a granddaughter! Talk about the agony and the ecstasy in one day. After two sons and three grandsons, we were delighted. We planned to go up and visit them in March of 2011 after the baby was born. My mother had planned to come from England at that time, so it we arranged it so that we would all go together. I had begun to think about what arrangements I would have to make if Alan had deteriorated to the point where he could no longer travel, but I decided to wait to see how things went until then.

Alan kept saying he would not go, which I now realize was probably a fear of being out of his own comfortable environment, but I was relying on the fact he would be drawn to the new baby, as the alternative would be impossible. He would most certainly have seen the opportunity of being left alone as carte blanche to spend every day in the bar. Or set fire to or flood the house. Or hurt himself. A horrendous prospect. Let alone the fact that he could no longer physically care for himself appropriately.

By late November 2010 we were sleeping in separate bedrooms. Sometimes I would lock my door if there had been a blowup. Alan was posturing aggressively then, coming at me and raising his fist, but always stopping short of actually hitting me. I would stop talking and walk away, which seemed to diffuse the situation. One time he snatched up the car keys and shook them at me, threatening to take the car out. Instead of saying, "No," I said, "I can't let you do that. It wouldn't be safe for you or other people. Just think if you ran over a child like Jack (our grandson)."

That did seem to stop him in his tracks, and he stomped out of the room. After that, I always hid the keys out of sight, but in a place where I could easily get them if I had to leave in a hurry.

That made me so angry. How ridiculous it was that I needed an escape plan from the man I had loved all my adult life. The man with whom I had shared tender, private moments, loved and laughed with. Sometimes after a tantrum, Alan would come and tap timidly on my bedroom door in apology. Often I would ignore him, and he would go back to his room. It sounds cold and harsh now as I write this, but I really felt that my husband was gone, and there was a scary stranger living in my house. My anger and resentment knew no bounds at those times. But I could not even argue with him. He had no concept of reason or discussion. I kept my feelings to myself. That was painful in itself.

On my birthday, November 22, 2010, Alan gave me a card that read, "Never from Always." Ever since we'd met, he was always very big on greetings cards. He would spend ages picking out the one with the perfect verse inside that said what he felt.

Strange as it may sound, I understood what he was trying to say: "Never forget I will always love you." I really loved that he had walked to the store and picked out the card himself.

Later that night in my journal, I wrote that on my birthday I felt "old, sad, and tired." I spoke of how much I had wanted to do in my life and how I had always imagined we would do it all together: travelling, dinners with friends, weekends away, and enjoying our grandchildren. I also wrote of how I had now accepted that my life ahead would be alone.

I still have the card as a memento of our great, enduring love.

Twelve

RAGE, BABY

The rages, mood swings, and irritability continued and increased. Nothing was logical to Alan, only his own confused thoughts. I was both lonely and irritated from dealing with the constant childish behaviors and the increasingly aggressive outbursts. Alan was moving further and further away from me, which left me alone and sad. That in itself was a source of anger for me, which then led to the inevitable guilt because I knew he couldn't help it. I wondered how long it would be before he physically attacked me. He would often tell me to "Get fuck (out) house!" And also "Shut (up), hate (you), bitch!"

He told me he got into fights with people at the bar because, "(They) don't like me." Neither was true. People generally avoided him and did not try to fight with him. His paranoia escalated. He was irrational and unpredictable, and he often frightened me during that time.

At Christmas 2010 we went to Los Angeles to stay with David and Lydia for the holiday. They had just moved into a new house and had plenty of room for Alan and me to stay. I had been looking forward to it with mixed emotions. Spending time with David and Lydia is always fun, and the four of us have had many happy times together over the years: trips to New York, Las Vegas, and Palm Springs, for example. We take it in turns to visit at home and manage about four to six visits a year. We had developed a very close relationship between the four of us and that would prove to be a wonderful comfort in the months and years to come.

I think David was quite shocked at Alan's deterioration and the changes in his behavior since he had last seen him in October when they came to visit us. Alan and David spent a lot of time together, but there was some nasty, violent behavior from Alan, thrashing around in a temper with objects, not people, and generally being obnoxious. I think he was so unsettled being out of his own environment that it led to a lot of acting out. Most of the time, however, things were calm, and we had a bit of fun. I appreciated the time that Lydia spent with me and that David took charge of Alan, so I could have a little downtime. I think David was a little afraid of the situation at that point, not really knowing what to do. He and Lydia were both so understanding and accepting. It is clear they truly loved Alan unconditionally.

For several weeks after we got home, Alan was completely convinced David was not talking to him because of his behavior at Christmas. (Yes, he knew he had done something, but not quite what). That was despite the fact that David had called Alan many times since our visit and had not mentioned it at all. Alan's speech and comprehension continued to deteriorate, but we seemed to be on a plateau for a while. Nothing really changed significantly. He had the same mood swings, irritability, and aggression, especially after drinking, which I could not get him to stop. If I didn't give him the cash to go to the bar, he would get aggressive, and frankly, it was easier to deal with him sleeping off a couple of drinks than to have to handle his anger with me for not allowing him to go. His friends at the bar were well aware of the situation. I had enlisted their help with keeping an eye on him. It worked out well, unless none of them were there, and Alan ordered his own drinks at the bar. I asked the manager if he would substitute nonalcoholic beer when Alan ordered and he refused, saying that he did not "think it would be right." I had my own response to that which related to allowing someone to drink who was already incapacitated. He would not help me, however.

At home I would find the hot taps left running in the bathroom and the kitchen. Alan had stopped watering the plants outside and did not always eat during the day. I had started leaving a sandwich for him in the fridge with the label "lunch" on it and a note by his coffee cup that said, "Your lunch is in the fridge,"

71

about three months earlier while he was still at home alone during the day. He was not even able to remember that by the following spring. He would take his medications twice or eat lunch at 10:00 a.m., because he had no concept of time. I made his coffee and set out his breakfast before I left for work. We had switched to decaffeinated coffee as Geri said there was some evidence that the less stimulation offered, the better in cases where frustration turned to anger.

His medications were in a "days of the week" box, but he would take Tuesday's and Wednesday's pills an hour apart, for example. I started leaving out just the current day's meds and hid the rest. Adam would call by the house at lunchtime to make sure Alan had eaten something. But I was making a meal every evening, so I was not too worried about him not eating during the day. He always managed to find the snacks and chocolate though.

In March of 2011 we travelled to Washington to see Chris and Amanda, our grandsons, and their new baby sister, Madison Paige. Our gorgeous new granddaughter had arrived on February 10, and we were anxious to meet her. We stayed in a hotel, as I thought that it would be easier for Alan rather than having to cram into Chris and Amanda's house with their three children.

"VISITING WASHINGTON, MARCH 2011"

Alan's behavior was even more bizarre than usual at times. Being out of his comfortable home environment was definitely challenging for him, and his behavior reflected his insecurity. Mainly he was confused about why we had to go and see Chris and Amanda every day and spend time at their house. He would ask me every morning what we were doing that day, but once he was reminded of the reason for our visit, he would be okay after a little eye-rolling and "tutting" while getting ready.

He loved the new baby. He loved cuddling her and cooing at her. "Girl, girl!" he would exclaim while holding his hand to his mouth as if in awe. We took some great pictures and video. They are wonderful lasting memories of them both.

"OUR FIRST GRANDDAUGHTER. HOW EXCITING!"

At dinner in the hotel one night Alan complained of being too hot in his sweater and wanted to go back to our room, which was some distance away. The door to the outside of the hotel had a keypad security lock for which one needed a code. I knew he would not find his way there or back, and I wanted to explain to the waitress that we would be right back, as we had ordered food. But Alan insisted on going alone and would not wait. He cursed at me loudly and left. The restaurant had large windows overlooking the path, so I watched as he went alone, took a few steps, and then came back. He could not open the door. I let him back in and offered to go back to the room with him, but he said he was okay now and didn't want to go. Being away from home was very stressful for him, but as long as I was at his side, he was a little reassured.

We went for many walks along the Columbia riverbank, which he loved. The river seemed have a calming effect on Alan. He always loved being outside, and he enjoyed those times thoroughly.

When we got home Alan spent the whole week drinking at the bar and at home. He walked around the kitchen one night drinking from a bottle of wine after I had gone to bed. He was making so much noise, I got up and told him, just as you would a teenager, to pack it in and go to bed. And he did. After that week he became much less aggressive, more subdued, and calmer somehow. That new tranquility was equally as frightening to me as the agitation and anxiety. One night I woke up in a total panic. I suddenly realized he was not coming back. Not physically, not yet anyway, but mentally.

My husband was gone, and someone else I didn't know was in his place.

Thirteen

TRAGEDY

By the spring of 2010 I realized how much housework Alan had not been doing. He hadn't been taking care of the pool, which had always been his pride and joy. He hadn't been doing yard work or cleaning consistently. The only things he continued doing were vacuuming and doing laundry almost constantly. I'm surprised we had any pile left on the carpets.

He expected a lot of praise (and reimbursement) for doing that. He no longer recognized the different denominations of money, and I wrote in my journal we were fast approaching the time when we would have to have someone come during the day to be with him while I went to work. One of the new things I noticed was that Alan had taken to pretending he was talking on his cell phone even when no one had called. The only words he said were "Yeah" and "Okay." It was as if he was trying to show that he still had connections and friends who called him. At that point he was sleeping for about ten hours at night and also napping during the day.

He had lost another bank card, which I did not replace. Instead, whenever he asked about it, I told him I had called the bank and ordered a new one, and then I said, "You know what those people are like." He would nod in agreement, and it would be forgotten for a few more days, and then eventually altogether. I surprised myself at how easily the manipulative words rolled off my tongue. My life was becoming more about self-preservation than accommodation.

FTD steals the contents of a mind, spins them around as if in some kind of tumble dryer, and then spits them out randomly, unexpectedly, without rhyme or reason. Alan was unable to do jigsaw puzzles anymore or work his MP3 player. So many of the pastimes he'd enjoyed were disappearing. The only things left for him then were watching or listening to something someone else had set up for him. When watching TV or during a conversation he could not follow, he would laugh inappropriately to cover up the fact that he did not understand. *Wipe Out* became a favorite. He would laugh uncontrollably while watching people fall over into water or mud. It made me sad and made me smile at the same time. I had taken to watering down the wine in the bottle in the fridge, eventually substituting it for alcohol-free wine. He never even noticed.

On May 24, 2011, we finally got to see Dr. Y. Our insurance coverage had changed and we were able to take Alan to the Alzheimer's Institute. Alan was pleasant and cooperative at the appointment. The neurologist made some medication changes and ordered a PET scan, which our insurance finally approved. Best of all, we got to share the resources of the Alzheimer's Institute: Geri and a social worker. They were so helpful and understanding. Adam and I later went for a visit together, and we were able to discuss the future and to start looking into what resources were available for Alan and us.

On Friday, May 27, 2011, at 5:15 p.m., catastrophe struck.

Our son Chris called to say that Amanda had found Madison unresponsive in her bed, and they were on their way to the hospital in an ambulance. About half an hour later, he called back to say, "She didn't make it, Mum."

Our darling, long-awaited granddaughter, Madison Paige, had died from sudden infant death syndrome (SIDS), aged three months and seventeen days. Even now as I write this over two years later, I am torn apart by the utter waste of such a young life. Tears of sorrow still come easily when I think of our lovely baby girl being gone. But I am so thankful that at least Alan got to cuddle her before she left us.

Obviously, when the phone call came, I was distraught at the horrific news. I was unable to control my reactions at first. Alan in turn responded to my reaction. Because he was unable to filter his emotions on the best of days, his reaction to the news was extreme. He became hysterical, throwing himself on the bed and alternating between screaming "No, no!," to sobbing uncontrollably and hitting the mattress. After about ten minutes, he lay on the floor in the fetal position and closed his eyes. At that point, I was completely unable to go to him and comfort him. I could barely even control my own emotions.

I made some phone calls, and Adam, Pamela, and Jack came over.

Jack said, "Why is everyone crying?"

We told him Madison had died and gone to heaven. He said, "Well, I'm sad too. I just don't have any tears right now."

Oh, how simple a four-year-old can make even the worst tragedy seem.

Once they arrived, Alan seemed fine and started to play with Jack and his toys on the floor in Jack's room. Later that night, when looking at the photographs on the table of all four grandchildren, he asked me three times, "Which?" and "What?"

He knew something horrible had happened, but not what and to whom. Eventually I pleaded with him to stop asking me about what had happened. I could not keep repeating it; it was so horrific. I think he understood from my tone that he shouldn't ask again. He never mentioned Madison again after that day.

In the months that followed Alan always associated the photos of Madison with our youngest grandson Zane when he was a baby. I think because that was how he remembered Zane before Chris and Amanda moved to Washington. When he eventually had a home caregiver, he showed her Madison's picture in a pink frame, and then pointed to a picture of Zane when he was a baby and indicated that it was the same baby. She wondered why a photo of a boy would be in a pink frame.

That night, after the devastating news and our emotional reactions, I waited for Alan to get settled into his usual night routine, preferring to keep things as normal as possible and not remind him or myself of the terrible thing that had happened. I called Lydia who, of course, was distraught too. Not just at the sad news, but because she was leaving the next day on a preplanned trip to England to see her father who was sick, and she would not be able to come and support us. By 11:00 p.m., I was able to call our family in England, my mother, Alan's sisters, and our closest friends, to break the awful news. I did not sleep at all that night. I spent the whole night alternately crying and talking on the phone. Alan slept peacefully all night, blissful in his ignorance.

How I missed having my rock to help and comfort me through the nightmare.

I have always been fiercely independent. I never liked to ask anyone for help, so when Susan offered to come out and take care of Alan while I travelled to Washington, I refused at first, telling her it was a kind gesture but I would figure it out. When I spoke with Lorraine, however, she said, "Let her come." After thinking about it, I knew she was right.

It was time to accept I couldn't do it all. I knew I would have to make elaborate arrangements to travel to Washington, and Alan could not go with me or stay home alone. I arranged to fly out early Monday morning. David would drive over from Los Angeles for a couple of days until their sister Susan could get a flight over from England on Wednesday. I told Alan I was going to a conference for work, and I would be in Denver for a week, which he readily accepted.

I travelled with a very heavy heart. Madison's death was something I had never expected to experience in my life. No one ever expects the death of a baby. My eldest son's baby. I wanted to hold him as I had when he was a baby. I wanted to take away the hurt I knew he was feeling. I wanted my husband to help our son and me to get through that excruciating situation. I wanted to help my husband through it. He did not need me to help him through it though. He was not even aware of what was happening.

I sat next to a man on the plane who talked all the way about his great-granddaughter's christening that he had just attended—pictures and all.

The pain in my heart was indescribable.

Staying at Chris and Amanda's house was painful too. There were reminders of baby Madison everywhere, and there were many people coming and going from the house. I knew I had made the right decision not to bring Alan, as there was no way he could have coped with the grief and sadness that filled the house, or all the people that gathered there. I felt very alone, never having had to handle such a traumatic situation without my partner by my side to share the pain.

Adam followed a day later, and we went through the terrible ordeal of the funeral together. Madison was in an open casket, as so many family members, including Amanda's mother and sister, had not yet had a chance to meet her. Adam and I had decided we did not want to see her, but when we walked into the church there she was. Beautiful and pale like a china doll, her favorite pacifier and dolly at her side. She looked so peaceful. Adam and I cried hard together for Madison, Alan, Chris, Amanda, Mason, and Zane, and for ourselves. I think Chris and Amanda found our presence comforting. I know Chris really missed his dad's support at that time. I also know we are all very grateful Alan and Madison had at least had a chance to meet one another a few weeks earlier.

While I was in Washington, I called Alan every day, sometimes twice. He called me many more times. I didn't always answer the phone. Later I would tell him that I was working and couldn't answer. Susan and David reported he was doing well but needed frequent reminders that I was away for work and would be back soon. During that week, David and Susan were exposed to how much Alan had deteriorated, and how he was no longer capable of making decisions or functioning independently.

David was alone with him for three days before Susan arrived. I am still in awe he did that for his brother. True love really does endure and knows no bounds. David's love for his brother leaves me full of admiration. I have known David since he was ten years old. I watched him grow into the man he is today. Alan loved him so much. They laughed, cried, and talked together. They also got into trouble together. They argued and got drunk together. They debated the merits of the various players on their team. They enjoyed the same friends and interests. It was brotherly love at its finest.

David left to return to Los Angeles on the Sunday I was due to fly home. Susan spent a very stressful day with Alan as she had told him I was coming back that day. A mistake, she later admitted, just like telling a five-year-old he is going to Disneyland tomorrow who then asks repeatedly, "Is it time? Is it time yet?"

He called me many, many times that day as I was between airports and flights. By the time I got home at about 11:00 p.m., Alan was distressed and tearful, anxiously waiting at the window.

Susan later said she thinks he was convinced the whole week I had left him and was not coming back.

Fourteen

DAY TRIPPER

Susan stayed for another two weeks after that. I was so grateful for her calm and comforting presence. Without Alan, she was my rock during that dreadful time of grief, allowing me to talk and unload my thoughts in our moments alone in the evenings. She stayed at home with Alan during the day when I went back to work. Together we agreed before she left that Alan needed more supervision in the daytime. She had spent a lot of time observing his behavior, and I was glad to have an objective opinion.

The night before Susan left, we had a terrible flood in our laundry room. It happened just before we were going to bed around 11:00 p.m. Susan and I did our best to stem the flow from a burst pipe while we waited for the plumber to arrive. Alan anxiously ran from room to room, unable to help or understand what was happening. He could not even follow simple directions such as "bring towels" or "get the bucket." He eventually gave up and went to bed. Susan and I were able to turn in around 2:00 a.m. after the emergency plumber arrived and stopped the flow of water.

After Susan left, Adam and I began discussing sending Alan to day care. As Adam pointed out, the very fact that Alan could not be left alone while we travelled to Washington was the key indicator that Alan should not be left alone during the day. He had a good point. What were we waiting for? An accident?

A flood? A fire? Or worse? He was right. We ought to be proactive and not wait for something horrible to happen. Leaving taps running, leaving the fridge door open, putting things away in strange places; those were just minor things that were daily occurrences. But the more serious things, walking around the neighborhood unaccompanied, riding his bicycle alone, and crossing the busy road alone to get to the bar, had become more concerning. We wouldn't let a five-year-old do those things, and that was approximately the cognitive level of Alan's brain at the time.

One Saturday morning I woke to find that Alan had gone outside and turned on the backwash for the pool the night before, and then left it on. Consequently, when the pump timer came on that night, it pumped out half of the water into our yard and the pool was half-empty! Alan had no idea that he no longer understood how to manage it but kept returning to old habits. We had enabled and accommodated his needs for so long in an attempt to preserve what little independence remained, but the time had come for a little more control to keep Alan (and us) safe.

With some help from the social worker at the Alzheimer's Institute, I found an adult day care center nearby. The manager, Carolyn, and the staff were wonderful right from my first visit. They welcomed me and gave me a tour. They listened to my tearful story and assured me they would take excellent care of Alan. They agreed they would go along with the ruse that he was working there, and I would provide a small amount of cash ($20) for them to "pay" him at the end of the day. I had told him I was working on getting him a job at a facility associated with the hospital where I work. He readily agreed that he would help other people at the center in return for a small cash payment.

And so, on July 5, 2011, a little less than four years after his diagnosis, I started taking my fifty-six-year-old husband of thirty-five years to adult day care two days a week.

The first day was a little like taking your kid to school for the first time. It was scary, tear-jerking, and sad. I sat in the car outside crying for twenty minutes after I dropped him off.

We got into quite a routine. I would wake him at 6:30 a.m., which he didn't like at all. When he stayed home alone he would usually stay in bed until at least 8:00 a.m. He would eat the cereal I had prepared, and then he would go to shower and dress. The latter two things took almost an hour. Sometimes he would shower twice. He would need prompting to brush his teeth and help with which article of clothing to put on next. The drawer opening and closing ceremony would go on for about twenty minutes until I went in and asked if I could help in any way, to which he would reply, "No, fine," and then finally get a move on after being stuck and not able to initiate moving forward in the process. I would drop him off on my way to work. He always insisted on just being dropped at the door (It was his workplace, right?). I would watch him in my mirror to make sure he went into the locked facility and then drive to work. The detour added about five miles each way to my commute.

For the first couple of weeks Alan would call me every so often to tell me, in his own way, he was finished and ask if would I come and get him. Typical of FTD's lack of insight, he did not think it odd that he was okay to go to work but not to drive himself there. It was another example of nonlogical thinking and the fact that he had accepted I would chauffeur him everywhere. Sometimes he would hand the phone to the caregiver and have them explain. He still had his own cell phone at that point, my nod to his independence, and a harmless concession. They would help him call my number. I would tell him I would be there soon, and he was okay with that. Then he would go happily back to the group and help the others he considered less fortunate than himself. He was very tender and protective with most of the other people in the group, especially the handicapped people in wheelchairs whom he took under his wing all the time.

One day Carolyn told me he had become particularly agitated, because there was lots of noise going on: the leaf blower in the yard, noisy activity in the center, and a new resident who would scream out completely unprovoked. Alan had picked up a large rock from a planter and held it over his own head. He'd done that in an attempt to protect Carolyn from a perceived attack by the gardener and other people outside in the yard. He had become very sensitive to crowds and noise. They were easily able to talk him down, and no one was hurt. The staff took it all in their stride, and there was never a suggestion that the behavior was inappropriate. Alan was lucid enough to try to tell me about the incident when I arrived to pick him up.

At those times I would nod my head and make all the right noises as if I knew exactly what he was saying. I never wanted him to feel as if he was being disrespected by me or anyone else. He was still my husband. I loved him, and he deserved to be treated well. The staff at the day care center all loved him. Alan would join in the dancing and singing, and he enjoyed it when I arrived to join in the dancing. We would jive and waltz around, putting on a show for his new friends. Then he would proudly take me around introducing me to people as "wife," shaking hands with the men and kissing and hugging the women as he bid them goodbye. Then the staff would give him the wages I had slipped them on the way in, and we would go home. On the way home, Alan would try to tell me about his day and ask me about mine. A vestige of our old life.

I often have cause to drive that way home from work now. Oddly, I remember those times fondly, and I smile to myself about the new normality that evolved during those days. Until recently when I changed to a new car, I would look over at the passenger seat of the car we had shared those times, and I'd imagine Alan sitting there, either being grumpy for some inexplicable reason or elated that we were reunited, time being irrelevant to him by then. Even just touching the passenger seat where he had sat brought back vivid memories of those days.

I would trade my present sadness for those past days, as turbulent as they were, in a heartbeat. Those times spent commuting to and from daycare were generally pleasant and calm.

This may sound strange, but one of the reasons the deterioration and constantly changing phases of the illness were frustrating and upsetting was because we all knew, ultimately, there was only one way for it to end. Dealing with the daily drama was exhausting; it felt so futile.

In my professional work, I have helped many families face the inevitability of terminal illness. But when I found myself in that situation, it was extremely hard to make the choices and decisions both for daily survival and for the short and long term. The long term was of an unknown length, just as it is for everyone. There is a finite point, but no one can tell you when that will occur. But when you know that it will be sooner rather than later—in the foreseeable future—it hangs over you like a black cloud, coloring your every move. Raining on your parade.

Joy and pleasure take second place to practicality and efficiency, no matter how hard you try. The caregiving life is just too complex to find much time for oneself, other than necessities. I cut my hair short, because I had no time in the mornings to style it. There were other changes I made in my life, but I never thought twice about doing them, because I loved my husband and wanted to spend as much time attending to what he needed and try to maintain some kind of dignified independence for him.

I did succumb to retail therapy, however. In the year before and some months after Alan died, I shopped and bought constantly. My wardrobe burst with stylish clothes and shoes. I bought things for the house, things for myself, and things for other people. I never thought twice about buying a version of something that was not the least expensive or most efficient. I just needed to feel in control of something. I resented the fact that we would never do those middle-aged things together again. I was making a good living from my work, and we would never get to enjoy it. It made me angry and resentful. We had always looked forward to returning to those days when we were first married, footloose and fancy-free, and enjoying life.

Alan's continued excellent physical health meant he was strong and fit. He still ate a good amount, although his food choices were very poor. A propensity for all things sweet prevailed. He no longer did purposeful exercise as he always had in the past. That desire was long gone. His work ethic remained, however, and he was very insistent that his workdays were always the same days he thought they were. He had no sense at all of what day of the week it was, so if he missed a day for some reason, it threw him completely.

Before day care, when Alan was home alone, I would leave him a note every day saying, "Happy Tuesday," or "Have a Wonderful Wednesday" and leave a lipstick kiss on it. I was reminded of that little action much later in our journey. So, if Alan asked me if he was going to work tomorrow, I always said, "Yes." I also sometimes told him Carolyn, the manager, had asked if he would do an extra day, as they were very busy and short staffed if I needed to change or add a day. If he was not going to day care, I would leave him in bed, go to work at 4:00 a.m., and be home by lunchtime, leaving his note telling him what day it was. Those three or four words would be about as much as he could read, and I'm not sure by that time if he even understood that. Adam would drop in for a coffee or to watch football (but really to check on him) in the morning while I was gone.

People who work with dementia patients and their caregivers will tell you at times of anxiety and agitation, memory lapses can come in pretty handy, and you can use them to your advantage. For example, resistance to a proposed activity can be overcome by changing the subject and then reintroducing it at a later time when the person has forgotten they have already resisted. There is also something that is jokingly referred to as "therapeutic fibbing," which is another useful tool to have in your arsenal. Unfortunately, one sometimes has to manipulate situations in order to merely get through the day with your own sanity in one piece.

After a while Alan went to day care three days a week. Leaving him home alone was no longer an option due to his understanding and judgment issues. I had a home caregiver (aka the cleaning lady) come in once a week, and Adam and I would tag team on the other day so someone was with Alan all the time. His old friend Bob Glass came to sit with him sometimes after the caregiver left until I got home from work. Bob would sit quietly in he chair, Alan busily running in and out of the room. Busy doing nothing. Alan once laughed and told me (in his way) the cleaner sat in the chair and watched TV with him ("Does nothing!"). But he did not have any concept of what was going on with regard to day care and home care and never being alone at home again. It was about that time that I started writing a sort of blog on a website that was recommended to me by a coworker, actually, my friend (and boss), Kathi.

CaringBridge (www.caringbridge.org) is a wonderful tool that you can use to let all your friends and family know what's going on as you progress along your journey. You can post pictures and your story, along with updates, as often as you like. The best part is, your friends and family can write in your loved one's "guestbook," and it helps everyone really feel connected. It was especially useful for me to keep in touch with everyone back in England, and they were very supportive via this medium. It also helped them feel part of the story while they were so far away. People would write the most wonderful things and post pictures and fond memories of Alan and our family. It was so heartwarming and comforting to me that they were all out there giving me strength.

CaringBridge also provided an opportunity for people who were not comfortable calling us on the phone or visiting to stay in touch. It also proved to be very therapeutic for me, as I could voice my thoughts and fears and know they would all understand. As I have looked back over both my entries and those of our family and friends, I am humbled by their comments about how strong and courageous I was. I said many times I was not doing anything that any of them wouldn't do for their own loved ones. To hear such philosophy and hope from the people I have known all my life meant so much, but mostly I was proud they thought so much of Alan that they would take the time to sit down and write a note.

During that time, however, I was also saddened and disappointed by the behavior of some of our closest friends. Thankfully, Alan was never aware of what I considered to be a hurtful betrayal by people who we had in the past never thought twice about supporting in their times of need. I have been able to let it go in the time since then. People have their own lives to lead. Their own problems, their own demons to fight. I know that now. What was happening to us was no more important than what was happening to them. My priorities were not theirs. I get it. I can understand and forgive their reluctance and fear of seeing their friend in his deteriorated condition. I can understand people have monumental issues of their own. Ours were mine, theirs were theirs.

There were some amazing quotes posted on CaringBridge, some of which I remember very well:

"When you reach the end of your rope, tie a knot in it and hang on."
—Franklin D. Roosevelt.

This quote became a source of connection and wry humor between Kathi and me. She too was managing a very difficult time in her own life: her father's terminal illness. We referred to the quote often, and I gave her a large knot of rope, which she kept on her desk for quite a while, as I still do with one of my own.

The FTD support group was also a huge help too as Alan's disease progressed. Sharing our journey with others who were at different stages of the disease was therapeutic for me and comforting in that there were people who really understood what I was going through. Sometimes I actually felt thankful and lucky I was not dealing with some of the things my fellow group members were, including sexual disinhibition, incontinence, lack of hygiene, compulsive eating, and weight gain, and in more than one case, ALS (Lou Gehrig's disease). I was grateful I could continue my work and still have Alan at home.

Fifteen

My Husband, the Five-Year-Old Boy

I am not sure at what point I truly realized I had transitioned from being wife to caregiver. I do know when that realization came, it was a revelation, almost a shock, in fact. Someone at the support group used it in a conversation with me, and I was taken aback that it was being used about me. Accepting that was a big hurdle for me to overcome.

The transition is insidious. Day-by-day the comfortable relationship established over many years is slowly chipped away in concert with the mental capability of your loved one. One of the most devastating aspects of frontal lobe degeneration is, despite the changes in cognition, the intellect is not affected for quite some time into the disease process. So intelligent, bright personalities can hide many of their losses for a long time. Because you care for someone, your spouse, for example, in the loving sense of the word, caring for him or her in the practical sense seems like a given.

Surely you always cared for your spouse?

However, when caring takes the form of being the chauffeur to day care, for example, or cleaning up soiling accidents or feeding them, the role of wife or husband takes on a whole new meaning. Not only has one spouse become more dependent, but the role of the other spouse becomes that of parent rather than partner. For a couple like us who had enjoyed a lifelong partnership filled with love, respect, and individual independence that can be one of the hardest things to accept. For a couple who may already have a rocky relationship, I cannot imagine how one would cope. Dealing with the practicalities for someone for whom you no longer have those unconditional feelings must be very difficult indeed.

Through the rest of 2011 Alan continued to attend adult day care, and we settled into a short period of relative peace. However, there were days when he resolutely refused to go. One day after I gave up trying to persuade him and was almost ready to leave, he changed his mind and got ready, which made me very late. Then when we got to day care, he refused to get out of the car! I begged and pleaded, and eventually he went in. When I picked him up later that day he was fine; Alan had no memory at all of the morning's events, and the staff said he had been calm and cooperative all day. Another example of how no two days are the same with someone who has FTD.

During those days Alan was always happy to play with our grandson Jack in short bursts when he came over to visit us. In fact, one of my happiest memories from that time came in the summer of that year when Alan played and swam with Jack in his beloved pool for the last time. He had become increasingly afraid of going into the water, and I had been unable to persuade him to swim with me. It was very strange. Alan loved his pool, and he was an excellent swimmer. He had always loved to swim laps every day for exercise, and we had spent many weekend afternoons in prior years, swimming together or sharing our pool with friends.

But that day he seemed more like the old granddad, laughing and splashing with Jack. They both enjoyed the time thoroughly, and thankfully I took a video and pictures to record the event. By that time Jack had become a little unsure of his granddad. Alan's speech was difficult for him to understand. But also Jack seemed to recognize Alan's unpredictability. I never left them alone together.

In August 2011 we travelled to Los Angeles to see David and Lydia. Alan was anxious but overall very cooperative and pleasant. Packing was a little challenging. For every T-shirt I put in, Alan took it out and put two back. He was unable to make decisions about what to take, so I suggested instead of giving him choices.

Choices are too hard for a person with FTD. He went along with what I said, even saying, "You do it," at one point. More chipping away of his independence.

We had a good time in Los Angeles hanging out with old friends, pulling the "old switcheroo" with Alan's beer and wine for the nonalcoholic variety. Alan had no idea and enjoyed himself thoroughly. We made arrangements for David and Lydia to come to Arizona for the New Year. Along with Chris and Amanda and their boys, Adam, Pamela, and Jack, we decided we would make what could be the last Christmas we would all be together a very special one. I was aware that we were entering the late stage of Alan's illness, and I tried to explain that to our family. The Christmas plan came as a shock when I told them the reason I was suggesting it, but I knew that Alan might not make it until the Christmas the following year. I voiced as much to Chris, although I don't think any of them believed me even then. Perhaps they just didn't want to. Chris remarked later about how prophetic my statement was.

On the way home from Los Angeles, at Burbank airport, Alan whispered, "Where are we going?" I reassured him we were going home. He nodded in understanding but asked me the same question three more times as we waited to check in. He tried to pick up someone else's carry-on luggage even though we didn't have any. Most people were very kind and understanding, especially the security people at the airport. I always carried a card to give to people that explained about his illness and asked for their patience. It worked very well.

Back in Arizona Alan was glad to be home, and when I went out to the store to get milk, he was already mopping the kitchen floor and had a load of laundry in before I got back!

Later that summer we went bowling. It was a pastime Alan had always loved and been very proficient. I was trying my best to spend more quality time with him at the weekends, but I was so exhausted from my busy workweek and caring for him that it took a mammoth effort on my part to be up for doing anything but lying on the couch.

At the bowling alley his scoring was not good, but he didn't seem to notice and enjoyed it anyway. He had always been very competitive, but that streak had long since dissipated, and he just seemed to enjoy the physical activity of which he was still so very capable. Alan was always so fit and healthy. It was a cruel twist that his mental capacity was so significantly afflicted. While we were bowling, Alan tried to wander over into the next lane a few times, but he was easily redirected. He also turned to face me at one point, ball in hand, ready to "bowl me over." When he saw me in front of him, he froze and did not know what to do, but again, he was easily redirected. The "freezing" stance is another common symptom of FTD. It was almost as if someone had pressed the pause button.

That evening, on the advice of Dr. Y., I gave Alan his first dose of Namenda, another drug widely used in dementias but with varying degrees of efficacy. The next morning we watched the final day of one of Alan's favorite sporting events, the Tour de France cycle race. He was thrilled that an Englishman, Mark Cavendish, won the coveted green jersey for winning the most sprint legs of the races. It was to be the last time Alan would have even a vague grasp of what was happening in the competition. Even then, he would get up and wander away during the program. Another favorite gone forever.

Throughout the next few days several of what appeared to be side effects of the Namenda began to be apparent: hot flashes, increasing episodes of being glued to the spot, wandering aimlessly, sweating profusely, and confusion. He could not carry out tasks at which he had previously been very proficient, but more importantly, he seemed to have gone back in time as far as speech and cognitive awareness were concerned. He was able to say four or five words together and even a few sentences again. However, Alan became increasingly agitated and restless, and a symptom that had started some time before, myoclonus, got much, much worse.

Myoclonus is a jerking or twitching of muscles caused by intermittent nerve signals. It was very distressing for Alan. It was a little like the jerk experienced sometimes just as you are falling asleep and something startles you. It had been happening to Alan on and off for about two years but got much worse while he was taking Namenda.

One morning a few days after he started taking the Namenda he made sarcastic comments and laughed at my road rage while driving to day care. Even before Namenda, after he stopped driving, Alan always made me keep two hands on the wheel. He would physically replace a hand that may have been down at my side and reproach me for bad driving.

I shared those observations with Dr. Y. during an appointment. By that time Alan had been for a PET scan. Dr. Y. said that the scan showed additional early-onset Alzheimer's disease, but since all Alan's symptoms were classic for FTD, it was likely both diseases were present. By that time Alan was unable to sign his name, follow the storyline of a movie he had not seen before, or tell the doctor the name of the current president, the time, day, date, or year. It had been just four years since our first visit to a neurologist with word-finding issues.

The improved cognition that may have been generated by the Namenda significantly increased Alan's frustration with his inability to carry out simple tasks. He was more aware of all the things he was unable to do. He became more aggressive and agitated at the slightest irritation.

One day, after three days of trying to fix his bicycle, he came to me with the broken pump and asked why it had not been fixed or replaced. I didn't even know it was broken. He had ignored the bike for more than three months. When I explained that I had been at work all day, he threw the pump at me, shouting, "Get now!" I moved away and ignored him. I left the room and he calmed down.

A little later Adam came over with Jack, who was supposed to be staying with us for a couple of hours. I was explaining what had happened when Alan came into the room and told Adam to leave ("You go!"), as he needed to talk to me alone. He was very angry and aggressive, fists clenched, and red in the face. Of course Adam would not leave us, and Alan started yelling about the bicycle pump again. I left with Jack and went to the movies. Adam left shortly afterwards. When I returned Alan was perfectly calm and asked if I had a nice time. He had no recollection of what had happened before.

We went to the store a few days later to get a new pump, even though I knew he did not know how to use it anymore, and he was never going to ride his bicycle again. He was unable to choose one of course, so I just picked any old one. Alan left the store a happy man and tranquility resumed. He stood and watched while I pumped up the flat tire to his satisfaction. He never used the pump or rode the bicycle again. The things we do for peace.

Adam has since told me that during that period of time he would dread every text or phone call, fearing I was calling to tell him something very serious had happened to either his dad or me. He worried Alan would hurt me or do something dangerous to put himself in jeopardy. He knew I would call for help if something happened that I could not handle. I hate that he was so troubled. I often feel guilty I leaned on him so heavily.

Every day Alan and I played "hide-and-seek" with various things around the house: money, clothing, mail, and toiletries. Alan would complain he couldn't find something or just be searching and could not tell me what he was looking for. I found shampoo and many other inappropriate things in the kitchen cabinets. I would just return them to their correct places. I found the bicycle padlocked to the bed in the guest room. Alan had taken to hanging things, a belt, a tie, and towels, from the curtain rod in his bedroom. He placed his boots outside in the yard and filled them with rocks. He filled the mop bucket with rocks, too, and left it outside the door.

I had by then completely substituted his wine for the nonalcoholic variety, and he didn't notice. His friends at the bar also made sure he was not drinking alcohol there either, ordering nonalcoholic beer for him. So he still had all of the social pleasure of drinking, and I had none of the pain. But Alan's daily anger and frustration continued. I never knew what kind of a reception I was going to get at the end of each workday.

It was exhausting.

Throughout his life, Alan had always keenly followed many sports: golf, boxing, athletics, anything really. He could always strike up a conversation with anyone about any sport. Even if he didn't particularly like a sport, he always knew at least the basics about it. His passion, though, was football (soccer). He coached it, watched it, played it, loved it. His favorite team, Manchester United, is successful and famous all over the world, and Alan was always eager to be involved in their success, attending charity functions and networking with people who were associated with the club in some way. He and his friend Steve attended many matches and championships together.

By spring of 2011 Alan had lost all interest in football. Since moving into our house in 2000, we had built a tradition for Saturday or Sunday mornings, depending on which day the game was aired live. Before FTD, we would get up, often at 4:00 a.m., to watch a live game and have a typical English breakfast. In those earlier days we would be joined by friends, ours and/or Adam and Chris's, and it would be a full morning of football, football, football. Unfortunately, in the midst of his FTD, Alan could no longer follow the game at all. To Adam's dismay, Alan would often get up in the middle of a game and wander around the house, always looking for something. He was totally unable to focus for more than about ten minutes at a time. The friends no longer came to games. Adam still came over to watch the midweek games during the day, but he was increasingly saddened by Alan's inability to enjoy the game anymore.

In FTD, passion is overcome by obsession. But sadly, not obsession for past passions.

We had walked together for exercise for several years. In years gone by Alan would run ahead and then run back to me. In the middle stages of his FTD we continued this habit in and around our neighborhood. Alan always enjoyed those times. Sometimes he would walk a little way ahead, and sometimes he would hold my hand. We had fallen into an easier way then. We would walk in reflective silence, each of us enjoying the togetherness. I treasured each walk, determined to hold them in my memory.

Taking naps was also very popular with Alan at that time, but I'm not a napper, never have been, so I used the time to take care of domestic bliss: chores. It was a time of great apprehension on my part, as I knew that new phases were around the corner.

By then, Alan had been evaluated by the state for assistance with financing the inevitable medical expenses I knew were coming. I also knew I would not be able to afford the residential care that Alan was going to need in the not-too-distant future. I was trying to be proactive in applying for help for him. He had been assessed by a nurse from the long-term care department (Arizona Long-Term Care System (ALTCS)) of the Arizona Health Care Cost Containment System (AHCCS).

The nurse agreed Alan already met the criteria for residential care, which was somewhere between needing mere "supervision" and more skilled "acute care." Even though he was not physically ill, he could not direct or maintain his own personal needs. Therefore, he would qualify. At that time Alan could not tell the nurse the date, day, time, or his address or phone number. It was not just because of his aphasia anymore, but because he really did not know. He needed prompting and/or direction to eat, bathe, dress, and toilet himself, although he could still physically carry out those tasks.

I was paying out of pocket for day care and the home caregiver at a rate of $10 and $20 per hour respectively. Plus, I was paying Alan a $20 a day wage to go to day care. I used to look for the cash in his room, and I was sometimes successful in removing it and giving it back in his wages the next day, as he had no idea how much he actually had. I even bought fake money from a children's learning center and added that into his real cash and he never noticed.

I was often asked during that time if we had any kind of long-term care insurance. I know that it is an option many people are taking nowadays, but frankly, since we were only in our early fifties, I was just thinking about beginning a plan, not using one. I guess we all think we won't need it until we're at least in our seventies and generally start paying premiums around age fifty plus. Sadly it was too late for Alan. No underwriter would accept him after diagnosis, of course.

By October he had $60 in his petty cash fund. He guarded it well; so well, in fact, we had to look for it three or four times a day. I soon learned he'd hide it in one of three places, so after that the problem was easily resolved. While searching one day I peeked into the bathroom while Alan was showering. He was always very private about that. He was washing his hair with shaving cream, but at least he was bathing. He often forgot to brush his teeth and would do it when reminded, but he was not yet at the stage where he would let me do it for him. When I woke him in the mornings for day care with a cheery "Good Morning!" I would often get the response "Go way!"

I used to think "How nice to be appreciated."

It was an exhausting time for all of us. Alan often could not settle or relax, and he would wander and pace in and out of rooms in the house. He would endlessly rearrange clothes and things in the bedroom. The only time he was happy to sit was if I would sit with him and hold his hand until he fell asleep. But the minute I moved or got up, he would be up again, being busy. He would ask Chris when he called, "When? When?," meaning "When are you coming to visit?" Chris would always tell him, "Soon, Dad, soon." Unbeknown to Alan, Chris and Amanda planned to visit at Christmas with their children.

Alan's speech had deteriorated enormously by that point. He was barely able to put two words together anymore. Phone conversations were almost impossible, although he always liked hearing familiar voices with me interpreting the calls and his responses. Some people just stopped calling.

That hurt. Not him, but me.

At the end of October we went for an appointment with Geri. She had not seen him since May, and she saw a huge difference and deterioration. She assessed Alan using the Mini Mental State Exam. It is a fairly quick assessment of cognition and memory. For example, the test asks the patient to draw a clock face. Alan's drawing consisted of a circle with some numbers on the right-hand side (not the correct ones), and the remainder written in a childlike scrawl in a wobbly line across the top of the page. He was unable to repeat three words, (table, pen, and flower) that were said to him at the beginning of the test when asked to recall them five minutes later.

The maximum score on the test is thirty. You or I would probably score twenty-seven to twenty-eight.

Alan's score was five.

Geri suggested the next level of medication, a low dose of an antipsychotic — Seroquel, which would help to keep Alan calm and less agitated. He was exhausting himself with his constant moving around the house, cleaning and tidying.

I was slowly getting used to sitting in the house, the car, everywhere in total silence as Alan's speech gradually disappeared. I'm a talker, and he was a talker. I was constantly grateful for the escape of my work and the support and encouragement I got there. It was an oasis, a place where I did not have to make decisions about mundane domestic things. I had to make decisions about other things of course, but they were related to other people's needs and not mine or Alan's. The list of things Alan was unable to do got longer and longer every day.

By that time he never asked about or referred to anyone he could not see, such as our friends, his sisters and brother, and his children and grandchildren. It was a case of out of sight, out of mind. He would frequently ask what day it was and verbalize thoughts using "word salad," which was a long string of unintelligible words. He rarely used my name, and when addressed by his own name, Alan once laughed and said to me, "You…don't call me that," as if he were surprised to be called Alan.

He did from time to time still compliment me on my appearance.

"Look nice."

I still got a kick out of that.

He would not wear new clothing, preferring instead his favorite yellow or orange T-shirts, which he changed at least four or five times daily, and laundered many times a week. They didn't last long, but I bought them in threes so we never ran out. He would only wear the same four pairs of underwear, so I bought multiples of those too. When getting dressed, Alan would stand motionless in front of the mirror, unable to initiate any kind of movement in a freezing stance. He was mesmerized by the reflection. Often FTD patients think that their reflection is someone else. They sometimes even go as far as trying to attack their reflection as they think an intruder is in their house. It can make them very afraid.

He would go through drawers, removing the contents relentlessly. I would have to prompt him as to which piece of clothing to put on next, and which way the clothing should go. I was still desperately trying to maintain some kind of independence for him by offering help but not taking over. If his bed sheets needed to be changed and washed, I would have to do it surreptitiously, as Alan did not like them to be disturbed. He would arrange his four pillows vertically, leaning them upright against one another across the bottom of the bed in an inverted "V" formation.

At that time Alan was fifty-six-years old.

Sixteen

OPEN WIDE PLEASE

*G*oing to the dentist—not an experience any of us relish I'm sure.

In October of 2011 Alan was complaining of a toothache, pointing at a place at the back left hand side of his mouth. He could not describe or explain it but would merely open his mouth and point. I took him to our family dentist to whom Alan was well known. The staff was very kind and accommodating to Alan's inability to speak. Dr. G. referred Alan to a surgeon for removal of the offending tooth, which was a wisdom tooth impacting the adjacent molar. I ran the whole scenario by Susan's son, Sam, who is a dentist and oral surgeon, for his opinion and advice. We agreed that extraction would be the best thing, but I was very concerned about Alan's ability to understand the process, his reaction to the anesthesia, and about dealing with his pain postoperatively.

Of course I did not want Alan to have the continued pain of the wisdom tooth either, so, after talking with the family and Geri, I decided to go ahead with the surgery. We went to the surgeon's office on November 11, and once Alan was under the anesthetic, I left the office and went home to wait for the call to tell me he was ready to come home. When I returned Alan was cooperative and pleasant, if a little bewildered, with the staff at the surgeon's office and the procedure went well. Once at home Alan went to bed and slept the rest of the day and that night without incident.

Little did I know the surgery was to be the catalyst for a whole new chain of events, which would be the biggest challenge we had ever faced. The recovery period from his dental surgery turned out to be painful for Alan and frustrating for me. He could not remember the dental surgery and that he could not eat solid food for the first couple of days. So I would find him helping himself to whatever he could get his hands on, regardless of its texture. Then he forgot not to eat on the left side of his mouth, so he would feel more pain that way.

Alan would only let me change the dressings infrequently, but he did readily accept the pain medication when it was due. Over the next few days, he developed a dry socket, which meant that a protective blood clot had not formed over the hole in his gum, because the wound had been disturbed so much. It was very painful, and Alan was not able to understand at all what was going on. I did my best to explain, medicate, and comfort him, but it was all very distressing for both of us. He seemed a little more confused than usual, standing in front of the mirror, toothbrush in hand but not knowing what to do with it until prompted.

It was the same with the shaving razor and taking pills. He held them in his hand but could not take the initiative and move his hands or arms. It was as if he was stuck. One morning he finally accepted help from me and let me brush his teeth gently and wash his face. He even let me wash him in the shower.

I cried so hard that day. I knew that his acceptance of physical help could only mean one thing: it was truly the beginning of the end. It was though we had suddenly jumped from one phase to another overnight, without any subtle deterioration. And there was no going back.

Alan was probably only understanding less than one quarter of what was being said to him at that point. The pain made him angry and aggressive. I started the Seroquel Geri had prescribed just before his surgery. It did help a little, and so I decided I would return to work after the weekend.

On Saturday night, November 19, my worst fears began to take shape. Alan became very agitated and aggressive to the point where I had to leave the house, as I was afraid for my own safety. He had thrown a plate at me while we were doing dishes together and had generally been argumentative. He was yelling at me angrily. I always made a point to keep something, the kitchen island, or the couch for example, between us at those times. I also made sure that I had my cell phone and car keys in my pocket, my purse nearby, and easy access to a door. It is impossible and pointless to argue with an FTD patient. He has no rationality or reason.

That night, when I returned after driving around the neighborhood for an hour or so, Alan was sitting quietly watching TV and behaving as though nothing had happened.

I felt alone and helpless. No one saw those episodes. But I am glad to say everyone believed me when I told them. Some people don't have that luxury. Sometimes even family doubts you are doing the right thing. Not ours, I'm happy to say.

The next day our good friends John and Amanda came to visit. They had not seen Alan for a while, so I had prepared them to expect some deterioration. They had been our friends for a long time and also our Friday happy hour partners in the days when we went out and actually had fun. Of course, being the contrary person he was, Alan was all sweetness and light, and greeted them with smiles and hospitality, offering coffee and even making a joke about being glad when they declined. The conversation went like this:

"C-c-coffee?"

"No, thank you."

"Good!"

It ended with Alan laughing at his own joke. We all laughed. Alan was animated and happy, and his behavior made me out to be quite the liar about his condition.

After John and Amanda left I made Alan some scrambled eggs, which he enjoyed at first, as they were nice and soft for his still-sore mouth. I then told him I was going out to the store and would be back in about half an hour. He completely lost all composure and became very abusive, swearing, and screaming, "Fuck! Out!"

Then he threw the bowl of eggs at me. In hindsight, I wondered if he was scared of being alone or abandoned.

I was scared and shocked at the sudden turn in his mood. I left in a hurry and drove over to Adam's house nearby. Adam came back to the house with me to find Alan still extremely agitated. He had changed out of his house clothes into jeans, a sweater, and shoes, ready to go out. I had called our nurse practitioner, Geri, on the way home and asked her advice. She said I should take Alan to the emergency room as soon as possible for an evaluation. Such a significant change in behavior could indicate something more acute going on, such as an infection.

By the time we got back to the house, Alan would not do anything I asked, even though I begged him to come to the hospital with me. Adam stood there with a look on his face I had never seen before, nor ever wish to see again.

Disbelief, shock, and fear were etched on his face. He was stunned by his dad's behavior. Neither of us had ever seen him like that before. Adam still says to this day that it was a moment he will never forget. It was a moment that changed everything.

Alan agreed to go with Adam to the hospital but kept pointing at me and shouting with gritted teeth and a thunderous expression on his face, "Not her, not her!" He did not even want me to go with them. I have no idea what was going through his mind then. He was so afraid. I sat quietly in the back of the car. Adam drove and Alan did not seem to notice I was there. He even attempted his version of small talk, one word at a time, with Adam as they sat together in the front seats on the way to the hospital.

When we arrived at the emergency room, he kept shouting at me "No, you, no!" So I hung back as Adam took him in. Even though his paranoia and aggression were directed at me, I felt so at one with him. I understood how he was feeling; I knew it was fear driving his behavior. It still scared me though.

Once inside Alan would not let me in the room, and the staff called security, as he was so aggressive and combative. I knew most of the staff in the emergency room, as the incident took place at the hospital where I work. At first, they asked if he had been drinking, as he appeared intoxicated, but when I said "No," and explained he had dementia; they were immediately kind and understanding. I had called our friends Bob and Carole on the way in, and they met us there. Bob sat with Alan while Carole and I met with the social worker. Alan calmed down considerably while sitting with Bob. After the rage and belligerence had died down, he was tearful, afraid, and remorseful. He did not know what had happened, just that I was upset, and he did not know why. He kept saying "Sorry, sorry" over and over. And he cried, cried in fear.

Alan was assessed and did not show any signs of dehydration or infection, so he was discharged home on the understanding that I would contact Alan's neurologist the next day. The doctor also wanted to be sure I would be safe. Once I reassured her Adam, Carole, and Bob were very close by, she agreed to discharge Alan home. Alan slept soundly all night. I did not. Locked in my room, I was apprehensive and afraid. I knew my life as I knew it was over forever. Alan's life was about to take an irreversible turn. As was mine. The end was moving closer. FTD, the thief, had broken in to our life and stolen everything we had.

The next morning, I called Geri to inform her and Dr. Y. of the previous night's events, and so began the next leg of our journey, the foray into the world of psychiatry.

The Dance was turning into a frantic jitterbug.

Seventeen

INCARCERATION

*M*onday, November 21, 2011. Many phone calls took place that day, to Geri, the neurologist's office, the psychiatric inpatient facility where Alan was to go for an evaluation. I called my work, Adam, Chris, Susan, Lorraine, and David.

Geri advised that Alan should be admitted to an inpatient psychiatric unit for further evaluation. The consensus from the family was that I had to do whatever I thought was necessary, and that they would trust my judgment and respect my decisions.

What? My husband, Alan, in a psychiatric unit? Of course, there are some people who would not be surprised by that. Some people would say it should've happened years ago. That's a joke by the way.

There were no beds available at the psychiatric unit, and so, as Alan was calm and cooperative, I took him to day care, because it was one of his days to go. When I picked him up, they said there had been no issues. I told them he probably would not be returning. He seemed so calm that day.

It was the inevitable calm before the storm.

I was still almost speechless, because he had no idea what was happening. I could not, at the time, and sometimes still can't believe it came to that. Oh, the nurse in me knew it would happen one day. I mean, I'd read all the books. I'd seen all the evidence. I'd talked with enough people, but I still could not believe it was actually happening.

That evening, however, a different story began playing out.

There was still no word of a bed from the psychiatric facility. Alan became more aggressive and paranoid as he searched the house for something unknown. He was agitated and restless. He would not eat, as his mouth was still hurting. I kept my distance, making sure to give him space to do his searching. It was as if he was no longer aware of my existence. Eventually, he settled into his room, made a lot of noise with drawers and closet doors, and around 1:00 a.m. I heard him snoring and managed to get a few hours of sleep myself.

November 22, 2011 was my fifty-sixth birthday. Alan would not get up at first, his mouth was painful, and he did not want to get out of bed. He rose around 8.30 a.m., took his medications in some yoghurt, and was generally placid and pleasant. I, on the other hand, was fidgety and anxious. But I am a good enough actress that Alan did not seem to notice. Adam came over, and I spent the morning again making phone calls and faxing information to the facility where Alan would be going. I was trying to avoid the potential emotion of the situation by keeping myself occupied.

It took until 3:00p.m. for them to tell me, finally, I could bring him over to the hospital. Alan had been calm all day, and I told him we were going to a dental specialist, as his mouth was causing so much pain. He accepted that readily. Oh, how those lies rolled so easily off my tongue.

After waiting around all day, by that time Adam had to leave to pick Jack up from school. So Alan and I set off together from our house for the last time. His suspicion and mistrust only served to make me more sad and aware he was gone from me forever.

The nightmare journey, the "White Knuckle Ride for My Birthday," was the journey into my new life—*our* new life.

I became "the wife," visiting someone who had become a stranger. In the various institutions in which Alan would reside as his disease progressed, I became "the family," like those people I speak with every day in my work at the hospital. I was the one who asked questions about her loved one's progress. I became that family member whose hand I have held, whose story I have listened to throughout my years as a nurse. I held the power of attorney to make all the decisions about medical care and plans for what happened next. I was the advocate for the best, because that was all I could do for the man I loved.

When we arrived on the psychiatric unit, I was asked lots of questions. Alan was continuously looking more and more suspicious as the conversation went on. As had been our way for several years, when anyone asked Alan a question, he would always look to me to answer for him and that case was no different. However, at a certain point, he began to indicate he had a question and started to say to the nurse, "How? How?"

And because I had been interpreting and finishing his sentences for so long, I finished his question. "Do you mean how long will you be here?" I offered.

As soon as I said it, I could have bitten my tongue out right then and there. What on earth was I thinking?

"Yes," he said.

The nurse said tactlessly, "Oh, about two to three weeks."

To be honest, I wanted to slap her. She clearly did not understand he was not a true psychiatric patient with whom she could make a contract about acceptable behaviors. Her honesty and transparency were lost on Alan in his deranged state.

At her response, he stood up from the table, picked up his (plastic, thankfully), cup of orange juice, and threw the whole thing right in my face. He was shouting and screaming words that did not make sense, but the meanings were clear. He was furious with me. The nurse called for help, and Alan was taken away to his room. I broke down into tears, and we finished the admission process. I knew she did that kind of work every day. I do it myself. Her lack of empathy was astounding. She just could not wait to get through the process and move on to the next thing.

She ended by saying I could call on the phone, but I should not visit for a few days until Alan got settled, and they tried to stabilize him with medication. I left the building and sat in my car sobbing for a long time. My emotions were running riot. How could I leave him there? How had we got to that point? I wanted to run back in and bring him home with me.

"Let's forget about the argument and kiss and make up."

That's how it had always been for thirty-eight years. Only there would be no making up. No laughing it off. No kissing apart from a motherly kiss on the cheek when I left him at the various places where he would be living without me, without his interpreter. Without his comfy sofa in front of the TV and without everything he knew and loved.

I cried all the way home and all that night. I felt that I had betrayed my love, abandoned him. I'd left him in a place full of crazies. He didn't belong there.

I called every morning and every evening for a report. I logged every call and the report in my journal. That first night the nurse told me he only slept for about three hours.

About the same as me.

They said Alan was up pacing, being aggressive and abusive. He was yelling at the staff and trying to elope every time the door was unlocked to let someone in or out. He slept better the second night but woke up hungry and ate the newspaper in his room. The staff gave him food and he ate it all. His most agitated times seemed to be in the evenings. He would hit the walls, throw chairs, and be aggressive with the staff. The new medications seemed to help a little, and he had a psychiatrist on his case. Alan would spend his days sitting by the door, waiting to escape. He was successful twice, as he waited for the locked door to be opened as someone came in and then nipped out into the exterior hallway. The unit was on the third floor, so Alan could not get out of the building, and they always followed him immediately. At other times he would wander the unit aimlessly.

The social worker scheduled a case conference for the following Monday, November 28, to which I was invited only after I asked what the plan was. I would have gone anyway even if I wasn't invited. The communication was horrendous.

The medication finally seemed to be having an effect by that Saturday when the staff reported Alan had spent most of the time in his room, occasionally sticking his head out. They thought he was asking for his family. He allowed them to assist him with showering, and he took his pills crushed in applesauce.

He continued to be combative in the evenings, and the medication was being adjusted to try to alleviate that behavior.

I spoke to him on the phone on Sunday, our fifth day apart. Alan was tearful, and he kept saying "Sorry" over and over.

My heart was shredded. I couldn't think straight. My brain was like jelly. It wouldn't work properly. I have no idea how I got through those days and nights. Even now it makes me nauseous to be reminded of that place and those days when half of me was incarcerated in isolation, not physically but mentally. We were being kept away from all things familiar and safe. We were joined by our isolation, each being locked in a separate space.

I could not even describe the pain to my closest family and friends. It was like a knife being stabbed into my heart over and over again, to hear him cry like a child and not being able to help him at all. I felt so badly for him, but I knew it was the right thing to do. He asked when he could come home. I told him tearfully he couldn't come home yet, because he was getting too angry at home, and I was afraid he would hurt me or himself. He said, "I know." Then he said, "Miss you...kids...love you."

And then Alan hung up the phone.

Although throughout our marriage, Alan and I had been on trips separately, I had never lived alone. I spent more time by myself in my own home in those few days over Thanksgiving than I have ever done in my life. Adam, Pamela, Jack, and I went through the motions of the holiday, of course, but I was grateful for the time to reflect and regroup. It was good to take a breath, so to speak, as we moved forward into yet another new phase.

I was sick with fear. For Alan and for what the future held for us both.

On the following Monday Adam and I attended the case conference. We discussed medications and what was described as Alan's participation in occupational therapy, which I found strange. He had not been able to participate in the true sense for a very long time. They said he would join in at the morning sessions but not in the afternoon when I suspected he was just very tired and needed his nap. I also suspected they really were not sure what to do with an otherwise fit and healthy man who did not have a true psychiatric crisis. FTD is not schizophrenia or bipolar disorder. It is not a psychiatric illness.

Following the meeting, we visited with Alan. He was afraid, unkempt, and very tearful. He sat staring out of the window forlornly. I felt his fear. All that he knew was gone. After being in the loving security of his family, he must have felt so alone and scared. We had kept him safe and sheltered in his illness for four years.

The few clothes he had been allowed to take with him were folded in a sad, little pile on his bed, along with a pair of slippers belonging to his roommate. I know seeing his dad that way broke Adam's heart, and he never went back to that place to see him again.

I cried all the way home. We kept telling ourselves we were doing the right thing, but somehow it still felt like we were abandoning and betraying him. Later that day, when I called, the staff said after I had left, Alan tried to join in a game of football with some other patients and staff, and he was calmer, although he still wanted to leave. They continued to adjust his medications with some success, but the agitated, angry episodes in the afternoon continued. He got angry when other patients were being taken outside to smoke, and he was not allowed to leave with them.

I received a call a day later asking me for permission to insert an intravenous line as Alan's sodium level was very high, and they needed to give him some IV fluids to correct it. He needed some sedation in order for them to do it, as he was not going to cooperate with the procedure. Well, he was never willingly going to let them do that was he? Even if you understand what is needed, you're reluctant to get poked with a sharp needle.

I gave my consent and then spoke with the psychiatrist who was overseeing Alan's case. He said the medication adjustment would continue and we should probably start to look for a place for Alan to go in about a week, as he anticipated the medication adjustments would be complete by then, and Alan would be calm enough to place elsewhere. Following placement of the IV line, Alan needed one-to-one continuous observation to stop him from pulling it out.

The cycle of daytime calmness and evening/nighttime aggression, alternating with tearfulness, continued. Alan's verbiage was once again reduced to word salad and general verbal abuse of the staff. Having been on the receiving end of that many times in my work, I felt bad for them, but mainly I just felt sad for my darling husband.

December 2, 2011, was Alan's fifty-seventh birthday. He had no idea and opened his cards and gifts with an expressionless face and sadness in his eyes. He kept looking at me questioningly, but he did not have it in him to attempt to ask a question. The medication was clearly suppressing his emotions, both angry and happy. Alan's behavior remained unchanged up until his discharge from the hospital on December 9. He was forlorn and lost.

On December 1 Adam and I, on the advice of the social worker, had begun travelling around the Phoenix area to view secure residential places where we might place Alan. I had also connected with Nancy, a coworker and case manager with contacts in the community, who could help me possibly find a place for Alan in a group home. Nancy and I had worked together when I first started working in Phoenix. I visited one place with a locator, Suzanne, but it was a long way from both my work and home, and Alan would have easily been able to escape.

Another place I visited could only be described as a hovel. It was a dirty house with dirty residents and no sense of understanding. There was one person watching over four confused residents.

Good grief. I would take him home first.

After a couple of false starts at larger places where they could not guarantee either Alan's security or the safety of the other residents, we found a place in Mesa, about twenty miles from our house. The place was aesthetically very impressive: clean, and quite luxurious. Their RN assessor had been to the hospital to meet and evaluate Alan and to examine his medical chart. She said he would need close observation, had poor communication skills (that was an understatement), and was a high flight risk. She recommended Alan be admitted to their locked memory care unit.

I think I was so desperate to get him out of the psych unit that I overlooked some important red flags about the new facility's capabilities and understanding of FTD.

During our tour, we saw the residents from the assisted living part of the facility coming and going and enjoying the wide range of activities that were offered. The locked unit was quite a different story, however. There was a secure, keypad-type entrance door leading to a long hallway where the residents' rooms were located. There is a smell about those places, which is hard to define. Not quite urine or feces, not food or cleaning solutions, just a mixture of all four I guess. The hallway was lined with high-backed armchairs in which were placed several elderly ladies and a few men in various stages of napping. One man was pacing purposefully up and down the hall. I could not believe it was to be my husband's new home. I wanted to run away, screaming, "No! There must be some kind of mistake!"

Worst of all, no one was dancing.

Eighteen

MESA

It had been difficult to find a place for Alan. He was relatively young, very fit, and healthy. Also, we were still awaiting the approval for his state financial assistance. We had to pay his first month's rent, $5,000 in advance in order for the care center to accept him. We were quickly running out of options. Alan had to leave the hospital, so we placed him in the memory care center, as it seemed the best choice of the few that we had. Adam and I managed to get the money together between us. The executive director agreed they would refund our $5,000 when they received the money from the state.

We moved Alan's things in on the morning of his transfer, December 9. His room was unfurnished, so in the space of twenty-four hours, we had to find him a bed, a chair, a TV, and nightstand and take it over to the place. I wanted to make it as comfortable as possible for him. I took many photo albums, his MP3 player, with which the staff promised to help him, and pictures of our family for his walls to remind him of all of us. I included a picture of his hero, footballer George Best.

He barely noticed them.

I wrote on CaringBridge that evening "As hard as the last few weeks and months have been, today was quite the hardest thing I have ever done in my life."

It was the painful end of one thing, and the even more painful beginning of something else. I had times of utter sadness and despair, but I had no choice but to come to terms with it all.

The family was all here for Christmas and New Year as planned. We had hoped Alan would still be at home for the reunion, but it was not to be. We visited in small groups. Alan seemed to enjoy seeing the grandchildren, and we played ball in the activity room and games at the table with him. He attempted conversation, but we rarely knew what he was saying. I know he was very happy to see us and enjoyed our time there. After a while he didn't even try to leave with us.

It was a bittersweet holiday. All of us together for the first time in years, with one notable exception. The life and soul of the party was missing.

Over the next four weeks, I was to receive many, many phone calls from the facility at work, at home, on my cell phone, and at all hours of the day and night.

"Alan is lying on the ground and won't get up."

"Alan is lashing out at staff."

"Alan has pushed over another resident."

"Alan is standing by the exit to try to leave with the visitors."

And on and on and on…

They never had a solution; they just always wanted me to tell them what to do.

On Christmas Day, after we had visited in the morning, either the staff called me or gave Alan the phone after dialing my number for him, five times in two hours. After a while, the staff took to calling me from their personal cell phones so I would not recognize the number of the facility. They clearly had no idea how to handle his behaviors. I accused the director of accepting him purely on financial grounds. Their RN had assessed him and was fully aware of his condition and behavior, so why had Alan suddenly become a problem? They should not have been surprised by any of his behavior, as it had been well documented in the psychiatric unit where they had assessed him.

One day I was sitting in the garden with him, looking out at the Superstition Mountains where we had been many times. We were holding hands just like any other middle-aged couple.

Alan said, "Where this?"

I told him we were still in Phoenix, and the doctor wanted him to stay there for a while, as he was not well. He turned and looked at me straight in the eye, took my face in both of his hands, kissed me and said "Thank you" as clear as a bell.

Just rereading that brings tears readily to my eyes. He had not spoken to me like this for many months. It pierced my heart like an ice pick.

I can still feel his hands on my face and see the tender look on his face. Soft. His hands were always so soft. It felt such a 'normal' thing to do. We had not had normal for a long time. It was a sign he was still in there somewhere. It gave me so much hope. Not hope for life, for I knew there was none. But hope for the fact he still loved me. I drove home in tears that day as I often did when leaving that place.

The approval for his ALTCS insurance had come through (the same day I paid the $5,000), and the facility had been paid by them too, but I had not yet been refunded my $5,000. It took eight weeks, long after Alan had been moved elsewhere, and me standing in the finance director's office and refusing to leave until she got a check for me, before it was refunded. Alan did not qualify for disability, as he had not worked during the preceding two years. He was too young for Medicare, so basically, the financial plan was ALTCS or me. I have no idea what we would have done if he had been denied ALTCS. I have only good things to say about the process and the people I spoke with there. They were sympathetic and understanding. They were efficient and helpful. Hopefully everyone has the same experience with their government offices. I doubt it though.

The staff at the care center did not seem to realize Alan was not a little old lady they could bathe, feed, sit in a chair all day, change her diapers, and then put to bed at night. My husband was up and dressed and waiting in the hallway for someone to do something with him bright and early every morning.

Left to his own devices so much, he flooded his bathroom several times as he was shaving in the mornings. The staff assumed him capable of taking care of his own hygiene needs, but it was apparent he was just putting on clothes and not bathing unless I told them he needed help and then they would shower him. No one ever really seemed to understand him. They spent little time trying to occupy what must have seemed like endless, lonely days to him. I explained his limitations but also what he was able to do. He was happy to look at pictures and books with me; I did it every time I visited. But the staff rarely, if ever, looked at his photo albums, listened to his music, or played a simple game with him. They assumed he was able to help himself. I got the impression they did not know what to do with him, and they were afraid of him. They clearly had no idea about FTD—what it is or what it does to people.

The lack of knowledge and facilities to care for this increasing number of people is quite alarming. Our society is just not equipped for the epidemic of dementia that is sweeping the world. The Boomer generation will succumb to dementia more than any other generation before them. Or at least more cases will be diagnosed as dementia. In years gone by, it was just "Granny's gone a bit funny in the head." There is still so much mystery about FTD and other non-Alzheimer's dementias. But more is learned every day through diligent research and dedication.

I have massive guilt about that time. Should I have tried longer to take care of him at home? I would have had to give up my job, our only source of income. I would have been putting our safety at serious risk. Spouses have been attacked and injured, even killed by agitated partners. Maybe I would have had to defend myself against him and hurt him. I could never have lived with that knowledge. Should I have looked at more places? I know now that there was nowhere else for that stage of his dementia.

None of it matters now, of course, but the guilt and self-doubt still linger. I suppose one always wonders what one could have done differently.

We would sit and watch TV together at the memory care place. He was happy to do that as long as I would sit with him. I knew he did not want me to leave, and I never said I was leaving. I just said, "I'm going to the store. I'll be back in ten minutes." And Alan would say "Okay" and smile. Sometimes he would even walk me to the door and then turn and walk back down the hall.

That touched my heart like a knife. The fact he was so trusting and accepting of everything I said, even the lies.

On January 2, 2012, the care center staff sent Alan to the emergency room in an ambulance at 10:00 p.m. They called to tell me I needed to meet him there and he "can't come back." He was sent for psychiatric evaluation "on the orders of the RN on duty and the executive director." There were only three junior staff members on duty in the building that night, and they were clearly untrained and did not know what to do.

Chris and I raced over to the hospital to meet Alan. We found him restrained to the gurney, shouting and writhing around. A security officer was at his side. Alan was crying and did not understand why he was there. When he saw Chris and me, he calmed down, and we untied him. He lay calmly on the bed for the rest of the time in the ER. As he had no medical needs, and it was the middle of the night, the ER doctor sent him right back to the facility and told them they would need to handle it the next day. They did not want to take him back, but they had no choice. By law he had to return to his official place of residence. They could not just kick him out and make him homeless.

Despite medication adjustments and changes, the care center was unable to meet Alan's needs. On January 6, 2012, they requested a bed for Alan back at the psychiatric facility for further assessment and stabilization. While they were waiting for that bed, between January 5 and January 8, I received fourteen calls from the staff asking for my advice, many from personal cell phones. I called Geri to ask for help from her and Dr. Y., as I was really concerned that another move for Alan could be detrimental to him.

On January 9 I received several frantic voicemails and calls asking me to call back immediately, as things had got so out of hand. I called back and left voicemails. No one was available to tell me what was happening. I was about to drive over there when finally Peggy, the only licensed nurse on the premises, answered the phone. She was out of breath, saying that she had been "running away from Alan" as he had become violent, threatening the staff and holding a heavy object (a marble pestle and mortar for crushing pills) over his head, preparing to throw it at someone. I wondered why he had access to such a lethal piece of equipment.

An ambulance had been ordered for him as a bed had come open at the psychiatric facility, so they were sending him over there. Before I could respond, Peggy said that if I didn't want them to do that, "…then you can come and get him yourself and take him home."

I was torn between defensiveness and embarrassment at my husband's behavior.

Peggy could not tell me the name of the accepting physician at the psychiatric unit or any other details. Between 6:00 p.m. and 6:25 p.m., I made three phone calls: one to Alan's case manager at the ALTCS insurance company, one to the insurance company's twenty-four hour line, and one to the psychiatric facility, each time leaving a message. No one could tell me where Alan was located, what I needed to do, where I needed to go, or who else I needed to call. It was frustrating and upsetting in the extreme. I was distraught.

How could this be happening?

What could I do?

How could I help my husband?

Nineteen

ONE-TO-ONE

The next time I saw Alan, he was in the intensive care unit of a hospital, restrained and chemically sedated to the point of unconsciousness with an intravenous drug called Geodon. Geodon is a "black box" drug. A black box warning is the sternest warning by the US Food and Drug Administration (FDA) that a medication can carry and remain on the market in the United States. These medications can cause serious undesirable effects (such as a fatal, life-threatening, or permanently disabling adverse reactions) compared to the potential benefit from the drug.

Alan had been kept in the emergency room at the hospital for more than twenty-four hours. The only reason I had not gone to him was because they kept telling me on the phone he was being moved, and they would tell me when and where. They were trying for a bed in the psychiatric unit again, but Alan had to remain sedated as he was just too violent for his own and others' safety. Rather than wait for a bed there, the care center had called an ambulance and sent him to the emergency room again. A fact the staff had neglected to tell me.

Geri called me after she was informed of Alan's readmission and reassured me the violent stage would pass, and Alan might need to remain sedated until then.

In the ICU Alan was kept sedated. We would try to wake him periodically, but when we did, he was combative and thrashed around. He pulled at his tubes and lines, so he was sedated again. His nurse told me the only reason Alan was in the ICU was because he needed one-to-one supervision and that was the best place for them to do that. I spent sixteen hours there. At one point when Alan woke up, we got him up into the chair, and he was calm for a while. He kissed me and said "Aaah" afterwards. He had pulled out his Foley catheter (the tube put in his bladder to drain urine) earlier, and he needed to pee but was unable to stand. He was too weak and could not follow our instructions. He became very angry and combative again, so we got him (well, wrestled really) back onto the bed. The nurse sedated him, and I had to lie on top of Alan's legs, holding him down while the nurse inserted another Foley, and then, thankfully, the medication overcame him and Alan went back to sleep.

As a nurse I cannot even begin to describe what being the family member is like in that situation. I was almost speechless. The nurse in me took over the practicalities. But at home alone I was overwhelmed by the enormity of the situation. I have no idea how I kept going. I was on autopilot, I guess.

Over the next couple of days Alan was transferred to two more nursing units, still sedated and with continuous observation (aka a sitter). I spoke with the doctors and nurses many times for updates. I went in every day after work to visit. Visiting was not very fruitful as Alan was nearly always sleeping. I would leave feeling sad and miserable.

On Friday January 13, I received a call at work concerning Alan's "code status." In other words, did Alan want to be resuscitated in the event of a cardiac arrest?

I gave them a definite "No" and asked if there was a problem. The doctor said "No," but he was trying to establish a plan for moving forward as waking Alan up had not been successful without a return of the agitation, and we needed to decide on what to do next. He suggested decreasing the intravenous sedation and switching to oral medication, but as Alan was unable to cooperate, he would like to insert a nasogastric (NG) tube. This is a tube inserted into the nose and pushed down into the stomach, thereby giving Alan a route for absorbing oral medications. I hesitated. It was one of the things Alan had always said he did not want to happen, at least not for feeding purposes.

It's a big deal, an NG tube. In the ethical sense I mean. It's one of those things that is usually discussed when talking about end-of-life decisions. Feeding via a tube to prolong life is something everyone should decide for themselves, really. It's also a little traumatic to have one inserted and requires cooperation from a conscious patient.

I left my meeting at work and called Adam, Chris, Susan, and David to ask their opinion. We all agreed that as long as the tube was not used for feeding and just to get medications in that might help to calm Alan so that he could become more alert and off the sedation again, we would agree. I called the doctor back and we agreed that would be the plan. I visited after work as usual. There was no change in his status and no NG tube yet. I spoke with Alan's nurse again before I went to bed that night. Alan had awoken and been a little agitated, but he was given some IV medication and went back to sleep. The plan was to insert the NG tube and begin the oral sedatives and antipsychotic medications the next day, a Saturday.

So, imagine my surprise then when, the next morning, I received a phone call from the social worker on the unit, informing me that Alan was being discharged "later today." I asked who wrote the discharge orders, and he could not tell me. I later learned the order was for discharge *planning* not for Alan's actual discharge from the hospital. Later that morning, I received a call from a Dr. N., asking for a full history (yes, really, again!), and what Alan's baseline behavior was before that admission. We agreed he would discontinue all the sedation in order to assess Alan's current cognitive status without medication and start again. Then, if Alan could and would take pills, food, and drink, he would be transferred to a new facility where they would be better able to handle his behaviors. The psychiatric unit within the hospital said they could not take him as they could not handle his behaviors.

Dr. N. did not think Alan would tolerate keeping an NG tube in. I agreed. If, however, the violent, combative behavior were to continue, the only alternative would be to re-sedate him and consider hospice care to keep him comfortable for whatever time he had left. I was totally devastated by the news. I could not believe the end was so close. I completely understand how people get to the stage where they are unable to make these decisions. You just switch off, because you don't really want to decide. I watch people go through this every day. I help them make those difficult decisions. Now I had to make them myself.

That afternoon I visited Alan with a leaden heart. I sat by his bedside and held his hand. I spoke with his nurse, Lupia, who was very kind and a great listener. Alan woke at the sound of my voice, turned his head, smiled, and allowed me to clean his mouth and wash his face. I untied the restraints that were holding his arms, and he turned onto his side so he could face me. He continued to try to pull out his tubes and lines and then went back to sleep. The next day he was able to take a little Jell-O and applesauce by mouth into which the staff had crushed his medications.

I spent the weekend calling family and friends, talking and sobbing. The emotional stress was debilitating. I was physically and mentally exhausted most of the time. But I would not give up my fight to do what I knew Alan would have wanted, however painful it was for me.

During that time of changing over from IV to oral medications, Alan was alternately sleeping and being agitated. When he was agitated, he would kneel on the bed, rocking himself back and forth with the restraints at his wrists. He developed a urinary tract infection from the Foley catheter and several pressure sores from being restrained. Once the heavy sedation was out of his system, he was able to be up and around, albeit with constant supervision. He would urinate on the floor anywhere and tried to wash his clothes in the toilet. He paced his room and the unit constantly, hardly resting. His sitter and I tagged along behind like shadows.

A nurse from another facility called Maryland Gardens (MG) came to assess him. She said they would take Alan as long as his antipsychotic medication was oral, and he could pass urine without needing intermittent catheterization. The hospital staff was made aware of the criteria, and it was agreed that Alan would be discharged to Maryland Gardens Care Center on January 23.

I went and toured the Gardens facility and agreed to Alan's transfer there. It seemed like a suitable place. But having already agreed to an unsuitable place once before, I was a little skeptical that they could care for Alan. I asked a lot of questions to assure myself that it was the right place, and Alan would not need to be moved again. The nurse, Debbie, who showed me around and discussed the terms of Alan's admission, remarked, "We are probably only talking about months of care at this point, rather than years."

That was not news to me. As much as I hated to admit it, I knew she was right. I knew enough about Alan's condition to know that his behaviors were indicative of the late stages of the disease. It seemed then that my husband might end his days there.

Maryland Gardens was a quaint kind of place, having been an old motel built in the 1950s. It consisted of low-level buildings with the rooms opening onto a central lawn area divided down the middle by a fence. Each half was designated for residents with different behaviors: territorial on one side and wanderers on the other. There were shade trees, bushes, and a high security fence covered by a thick hedge all the way around.

I knew immediately Alan would like it (such as he could like anything anymore), as he had always loved being outside. He would be able to see the sky. At least because it was open air, there was little to no smell. They had a psychiatrist, a psychologist, and a medical doctor who would all collaborate in Alan's care. They seemed to have an excellent model of care in place and good resources for taking care of residents with challenging, combative behaviors like Alan. The staff was friendly and caring, and they seemed engaged in their work.

Discharge day from the hospital came. When the transport people arrived, Alan refused to go with them, so they left without him. They just accepted his refusal. They didn't even call me. It would be another twenty-four hours before he was discharged and moved to his new home. Unbelievably, the day of discharge, the hospital case manager called me and asked me if I would transport Alan myself as they were having trouble getting an ambulance.

I declined, needless to say. They just didn't get it at all.

Twenty

MARYLAND, MARRIAGE, AND MOVING

The first hour he was at Maryland Gardens, Alan slapped a resident, pushed his roommate, and was moved to another room. He was pacing and wandering, and he was very agitated. Of course, it was all understandable. It would have been distressing for any of us, let alone someone who could not understand or reason out situations. I had a long phone chat with Cleo, the nurse manager. She was very compassionate and reassured me they would take care of everything. I could visit whenever I wanted to, and she looked forward to meeting me.

Over the next couple of days, I spoke with Alan's doctors and his ALTCS case manager who had been in to see Alan and reported he had settled rather well. He was pleasant and cooperative when she saw him. One of my calls to MG revealed that Alan had hit out at staff several times and undressed himself outside, but as the nurse, Patty said, "That's why he's here."

What a relief. She reiterated Cleo's statement that they were used to handling those types of behaviors, and I should use the time to relax and regroup. I wrote in my journal: "I feel relieved but redundant."

Alan's condition continued to deteriorate more rapidly. His speech and physical abilities were eroding quickly. Each week something else disappeared. FTD, the thief, was at work again.

One Sunday when I visited he approached me in the garden with a smile and a hug. His walk had turned entirely into more of a shuffle at that point. His speech was mostly garbled with the odd recognizable word here and there. He was not sure which room was his, and when I took him there, he did not know which bed was his. He was being assisted into the shower one day when I arrived. I could not believe he was allowing two young men to help him undress and bathe. As he got down to his underwear, I noticed he was wearing his underpants inside out. I had to turn away and laugh. There, across the back of the pants in bold, black Sharpie, was the name "Richard Stewart" (not the real name). He had lost any sense of ownership or belonging. He wore other people's clothes, ate other people's food, and had no sense of what was his, even things that had previously been precious to him. I wanted to laugh and cry at the same time. My proud, private husband was in someone else's underwear, being washed by two young men. And he thought nothing of it as he smiled benignly and cooperated.

But Alan always knew I was his wife, and he would tell people that, in his own way, of course. I became "wife." Alan had not said my name for many years.

The staff was wonderful. They were very patient and kind. They always wanted to know more about him, and I got the impression they genuinely cared about Alan. They realized letting him sit in the dining room with one of them after everyone else had finished their meal, rather than making him sit with all the other residents who were very noisy, made for a more peaceful mealtime. Alan would eat more and be more pleasant without the cacophony of the others. I felt comfortable and happy that my husband was finally getting the care he so needed and deserved, but so, so sad that he was all but gone.

On January 31, I experienced happiness and sadness simultaneously as I watched our son, Adam, and his girlfriend, Pamela, finally tie the knot after eight years together. Alan would have been so proud, as I was, as they said their vows. I shed quite a few tears for their happiness and also for what Alan and I had lost.

In February I took a short break to go and see David and Lydia in Los Angeles. It was the first time I had been away alone since Alan had moved out of the house, and it was nice to get away and feel secure that Alan was safe and well cared for. He was settling in quite well. The staff was managing his behaviors, and I was comfortable about leaving him.

When I returned to Phoenix I made plans to move out of our house and into a condo nearby. Staying in what had been our family home for thirteen years was too much for me to take. The house was too large, too much work, and echoed of all the times, fun and not-so-fun, we spent there together. It felt good to have a distraction that kept me busy rather than sit and dwell on my lost life.

February 10 marked what would have been Madison's first birthday, so it was a somewhat somber time too. That, combined with the sentimentality of moving out of our family home and going through many treasured memories as I downsized our life, was so very emotional. But I could not face living in the house where we had shared so much together. I felt a little guilty as I got rid of so many things, but neither of us needed them anymore. I think that was what made me so sad: finally accepting that Alan was never coming back. I looked in every nook and cranny, every piece of furniture for Alan's wedding ring and gold neck chain. They had been lost for quite a while as he used to take them off frequently while living at home. But to my great sadness, I never found them.

Adam spoke of being "caught between hope and closure" at that time during one of our many heart-to-heart talks. There was no hope of recovery and no closure after a final event. Just a feeling of being in limbo.

The final day of leaving the house was February 29, 2012. Adam and I went over there together to pack the last few things in the car and to make sure everything was secure. I felt almost numb about it really. It was a little surreal. All our possessions were gone. Either sold or moved into my new home. They meant so little to me then. I got rid of things in anger and resentment.

I watched silently as Adam stood staring at the pool and the backyard for the last time, remembering the many great times we had all had there.

Watching him standing there, staring at the pool, shoulders dropped, and deep in thought, cut me to the core.

Alan continued to be relatively settled in his new home, and we established a new routine of visits. At first, Adam was reluctant to go. He hated to see his dad so changed. He felt powerless and helpless. One day he finally said he was coming to visit with me. I suggested we go in two cars so he could leave when he was ready. We set off and halfway there, he called me and said he was turning around and going home, as he could not face it. He said he felt a little foolish, but he would come next time.

Adam did eventually gather the courage to go, and he found it was not as bad as he had feared. We went together, and he stayed much longer than I expected. We talked a lot on the way home, and he expressed guilt, anger, and resentment at the cruel turn of events in all our lives. He was mostly sad to have—for all intents and purposes—lost his dad. He visited more often after that. One time he went alone. Alan walked right by him, not recognizing Adam until he tapped him on the shoulder and announced himself. Adam was naturally taken aback and very upset by Alan's reaction.

Another time we walked in together, and Alan rushed up to us with an "Aaah," squealing with delight, hugging and kissing us, and showing us off to the staff and other residents. It was quite the greeting!

"ADAM AND HIS DAD, MARYLAND GARDENS, APRIL 2012"

Alan would always have half-eaten, melting chocolate chip cookies in his pocket. He would take one out every now and again, nibble it, and then put it back. I would take him his favorite English candy, Rowntree's Fruit Pastilles or Reese's Peanut Butter cups, and he would share them with me. He also still loved his Starbuck's Strawberries & Crème Frappuccino. It comforted me to be able to bring those little pleasurable things to him, and he really appreciated them, if only momentarily.

Whenever I left him to go home at that time, I would again tell him, "I am going to the store, be back soon," or "I have to go back to work." If he got upset, I would say, "I will never leave you, I will always come back."

One time, when I said I was going to the store, Alan said, "Oh...come?"

I laughed and said, "Oh no, you hate shopping with me."

Alan laughed too and nodded and said, "Okay."

Sometimes we would sit on the swing seat in the garden and listen to his MP3 player, one earpiece each. He would sit quietly holding my hand and smile. Sometimes Alan would try to mouth the words of the songs, and then he would eventually doze off. I would sit there with tears rolling down my cheeks as every golden oldie song reminded me of a place or time we had been through together during our thirty-eight years.

Alan never noticed my tears or sadness.

As strange as it may seem, I treasure those moments of brief, relative happiness. The swing in the garden was an oasis of calm in our otherwise turbulent world.

"MARYLAND GARDENS, APRIL 2012"

One day when I arrived to visit, Alan ran over to me saying, "Never leave, come back." He'd remembered what I had said.

It was a fleeting moment, forever treasured.

Twenty-One

OFF TO MARAVILLA

*I*n April 2012 I felt secure enough in the knowledge that Alan was being well cared for at Maryland Gardens to go on a trip to England to see my mother who had been ill. Cleo, the manager, had said despite several attempts to regulate Alan's medications, he still had periods of agitation and aggression, alternating with calm and cooperation. The doctors felt that Alan still had some level of cognition and understanding, and they were trying to titrate his medications so he could have some quality of life. I argued with them that living in a facility like theirs was not any kind of quality of life Alan would ever choose, and they should stop. His physical health and young age were very deceiving.

I was assured his behavior was still within the facility's scope of care. They were still working with the psychiatrist and psychologist to manage Alan's behavior, but they had placed his name on a waiting list for the next level of care, which would probably mean one-to-one supervision they could not provide. Cleo did say that it would not happen very soon, so my trip plans should not be changed.

When I returned from England I went the next day to visit Alan. I had called for updates, and things were going about the same. I visited in my usual way. I talked with the staff who assured me nothing much had changed while I had been gone. I was somewhat surprised then that the next day, Cleo called me to say there was a bed available at the new facility. The place was on the far west side of the Phoenix Valley, about forty miles from where I live. I asked them to keep me updated and to let me know when Alan actually left so that I could go over to the new place and meet him there.

I have to admit I was more than a little irritated by the call. I had just been there the day before, and I was not given any indication the transfer was imminent. I called several times that afternoon to Maryland Gardens and to the new facility. Once again, no one could ever tell me where Alan was or what was going on. Finally, at 10:00 p.m., I received a call from the emergency department where Alan was being transported. The nurse said he had arrived safely but needed to be medically cleared in their emergency department before being admitted to the behavioral health unit. He was sleeping soundly, and they would let me know as soon as he was admitted.

At 10:40 p.m., I received a call from the emergency department social worker, asking me for medical history and other information. I received another call at 11:00 p.m. and another at 1:00 a.m., at which point I told them they may work the night shift but I didn't. I asked—unless they had something new to tell me, or there was a significant change in Alan's condition, or they needed me to drive over there—could it please wait until morning? They agreed and they kindly waited until 5:00 a.m. I received a call asking me to fax over the power of attorney paperwork and any medical notes I had. I faxed over the things they asked for, and they said that they would call me and tell me what room he was being admitted to so that I could meet him there.

A useful tip here would be to always have at least six copies of all your records available, including power of attorney, living will, advanced directives, names and numbers of all doctors, previous medical history, and contact numbers for family, because everyone wants to see them. In Arizona, not only do you need durable power of attorney and healthcare power of attorney, you also need mental health power of attorney. Even then, when the time comes to have someone involuntarily admitted to a psychiatric facility, you will still need a letter from a doctor (a neurologist, for example), to say that the patient is no longer capable of making decisions for him or herself.

So, in the midst of the storm of keeping everyone safe, you also have to deal with the official practicalities. You will need help from a friend or family member, believe me. If you don't have this paperwork, you may have to file for guardianship with the courts, which is a time-consuming and costly procedure. I would encourage everyone with dementia or not, to have power of attorney paperwork in place. You cannot assume that, just because you are married to someone, everyone will do what you say or want. Your loved one may even try to get their own attorney, divorce you, or spend all your money if you don't do this.

⁓

At 8.30 a.m. I received another phone call telling me there was no bed available in the Del Webb behavioral health facility, and they were transferring Alan downtown to another psychiatric facility for evaluation. Eventually, I found that Alan had been sent to a place about three miles down the road from Maryland Gardens in downtown Phoenix. Thankfully he had slept (sedated) through the whole thing, and he was not agitated at all.

I drove up to MG to pick up all of Alan's personal effects and then over to the new place. Ironically the psychiatric unit was housed in what had been the very first general hospital I worked in when we came to Phoenix in 1999. It was very strange for me to go back there after twelve years. The psychiatric unit, Senior Horizons (S.H), seemed comfortable enough. Alan was in a semiprivate room but that had been the case for the last six months, so it did not bother him. The unit seemed clean and light. The staff was attentive and friendly. There were activities going on all the time, but Alan was unaware and unable to participate. We would sit in the lounge area, and I would assist him with his drink. He was beginning to have difficulty swallowing and had to be watched carefully.

One time I visited and Alan was wearing what can only be described as a "onesie," a jumpsuit with no openings in the front. The onesies are designed with the opening in the back so that the wearer cannot remove it. I understood the reason for the garment. Alan had taken to disrobing randomly, possibly when he got the urge to urinate. He was unable to verbalize his needs, so a watchful eye was needed.

The only problem I had with the garment was that it was clearly intended for a female patient, being light blue with lavender flowers. Advocating for his dignity was really the only thing left that I could do for Alan, and I complained to his nurse. I took him to the bathroom, removed the onesie, and replaced it with his own T-shirt and shorts. The nursing assistant apologized and said they had no male garments available, but it would not happen again and it did not.

I visited most days on my way home from work and each weekend during the three weeks that Alan was there being assessed. Alan was very heavily sedated, and that was really the only way his behavior could be controlled. His swallowing ability was deteriorating, and he was losing weight fast, because he could not eat or drink very much. He was still able to shuffle around the unit, but most times Alan just sat in the chair.

Sometimes he didn't seem to recognize me. He did not speak to me at all. Other times he smiled, held my hand, and seemed pleased to see me. But he no longer knew whether I came or not or when I left. The facility had strict visiting hours and to be very honest, I was glad. I hated to see him that way. I was more than ready to leave when visiting time was over.

May 27 marked the first anniversary of Madison's death. I flew up to Washington to be with Chris and Amanda and some of the family as we lit candles and remembered our darling girl. A year had also passed since we had realized that Alan needed to be cared for outside our home. It was sadness times two.

I visited the psychiatric unit upon my return. The nurse asked me to wait in a small private room, and they would bring Alan in to me as he was sleeping in his room. The aide brought him in, shuffling, led by both hands. He was wearing a onesie (male version, no flowers) again; all that was missing were handcuffs and chains around his ankles. He looked like a prisoner.

His head was down, eyes closed. I put my head under his chin, looking up at his face. He opened his eyes wide and gave me the biggest smile I had seen in a very long time. But he could not lift up his head, a side effect of his antipsychotic medication. The aide assisted him into the chair and we sat there, side-by-side, holding hands, as we had done for so many years before.

Alan went back to sleep in his chair, and I sat there in mine with tears streaming down my face. I could not believe the body next to mine was the man who had been the other half of me for thirty-eight years.

I had many conversations with the social worker at Senior Horizons. She listened to what I had to say and was very helpful and kind. She suggested a possible next place for Alan and recommended I go and take a look at it, as he would be discharged very soon, and we needed to find a new residence for him.

"So, here we go again," I thought.

I enlisted the help of a friend and coworker, Linda. Linda is a fellow nurse, has been in healthcare for many years, and she has previously managed a skilled nursing unit. I valued her opinion and advice as to where my husband should be placed, probably for the last time. Linda and I drove over to the facility one afternoon after work. We were greeted by Ed, the administrative admissions nurse. He was very kind and friendly. He toured us around the large facility, ending the tour at the unit where Alan would be housed.

The first thing that struck me was that the unit was very well-staffed with several patients having one-to-one observation and care. The decor was a little shabby but clean, and the unit was lively and animated. The staff looked happy, and everyone came over and introduced themselves to us. There was a good vibe about the place. Linda remarked as we were leaving that none of the patients had food on their clothes, even though it was late afternoon and they had probably eaten breakfast and lunch before then, which meant that their clothes had been changed. It was a good sign that the standard of care was high. I am forever grateful to Linda for her keen insight and valued opinion and advice.

And so, on June 1, 2012, my darling moved into his final residence, the aptly named "Sunset Point" unit at Maravilla Care Center, Phoenix, Arizona.

I was not sure I was ready for the last waltz.

Twenty-Two

CHOPIN AND CHANGIN'

Music.
Musick has Charms to sooth a savage Breast,
To soften Rocks, or bend a knotted Oak.
I've read, that things inanimate have mov'd,
And, as with living Souls, have been inform'd,
By Magick Numbers and persuasive Sound.
What then am I? Am I more senseless grown
Than Trees, or Flint? O force of constant Woe!
'Tis not in Harmony to calm my Griefs.
Anselmo sleeps, and is at Peace; last Night
The silent Tomb receiv'd the good Old King;
He and his Sorrows now are safely lodg'd
Within its cold, but hospitable Bosom.
Why am not I at Peace?
—William Congreve, *The Mourning Bride*, 1697

$\mathcal{M}$usic has played such a large part in our lives. We always loved to listen, to dance, to sing along. Various songs and pieces made up the soundtrack of our lives. I can divide up the parts of our life just by naming a selection of songs that meant something at the time and still do. It's comforting in a way. It helps you remember what you were doing, who you were then, and how your life was going: happily or not so happily, ecstatic at the birth of a baby, or morose at the death of a grandparent. Music brings back memories of a trip, a Christmas party, or a wedding.

I could give you a list of music for each chapter of this book. That's how strongly music featured in our lives. But it wouldn't mean anything to anyone else. That's the nice thing about your soundtrack. It's personal and only has meaning for you.

Music marks the chapters in your story. Every time you hear a certain song, it sparks memories. Sometimes memories spark a certain song to play in your head. We kept a record player so that we could listen to our collection of vinyl albums.

Even into the later stages of his illness, Alan could still identify with his old Led Zeppelin LP's. We had an eclectic mix of rock and pop ranging from the '60s to the '80s when CDs took over. Later, we would listen on an MP3 player, and Alan would nod his head and try to sing along.

William Congreve had it right: music can be soothing and effective in the stirring of emotion or the alleviation of fears.

In 2011, I began listening to my local classical music channel on the radio on my way to work in the mornings. I found it really soothing. Then I listened on the way home and on the way to visit Alan. Finally, I had my morning alarm tuned to the channel to wake me up. I still do.

I find it calming and undemanding, unlike the usual popular music channels. They scream, "Hear me! Hear me!" The modern tunes bring memories or invoke emotions I do not want to feel right now. I can procrastinate and drift away to Chopin, Tchaikovsky, and Vivaldi.

I found I was particularly attracted to classical and acoustic guitar, and I discovered one then another, and then another favored artist: David Russell, John Williams, Jesse Cook, and Ottmar Liebert.

I can think or not think; cry or not cry. Classical music demands nothing but gives much. No words mean no need to listen. You can just let the sound wash over and around you.

It's a coping mechanism. Enough said. Try it.

It works for me.

Twenty-Three

LAST DANCE

Maravilla Care Center is located at the foot of South Mountain, the largest municipal park in the United States. The park is popular with locals and tourists for hiking, biking, and horse riding. It is a large, desert mountain space with hiking trails and rocky terrain. It's beautiful in its way. You have to learn to appreciate the attraction of the different desert species of plants and wildlife. It's close enough to hear the desolate howls of coyotes at night and find scorpions in your shoes if you leave them turned right side up in your house. Sometimes there are wild javelinas waiting expectantly for their dinner to be served when you put your trash out.

On the opposite side of the mountain to Maravilla is the home Alan and I shared for twelve years. The mountain is one block from our house. Alan spent many happy hours with his binoculars and without, watching the hikers travel along the top of the mountain, like ants on the skyline. We were among them many times. It seemed so right he had returned to live beside one of our favorite places to spend whatever was left of his life.

Before FTD Alan loved hiking and running the mountain during the pleasant spring, winter, and fall months in Phoenix. It seemed fitting then he should be cared for in the shadow of the mountain, with its landmark antennas being visible from the day room of the unit where he was living. Not that he ever noticed

136

them, but I liked to sit in there with him and look at them, fondly remembering happier times up there on the mountain, often with our visitors from England. It was one of the spots we always used to take people.

The day after Alan arrived at Maravilla David and Lydia arrived for a weekend visit that had been planned long before we knew Alan was going to be moving. It was good they would get to see Alan's new home and spend some time with him. We chatted with the staff who were extremely welcoming. They were eager to learn as much as they could about Alan. He needed one-to-one care twenty-four hours a day. It was the perfect solution to his needs. I was ecstatic to learn the facility was well prepared for residents like Alan, and he would have only a few people taking care of him directly. Consistency and understanding. Wonders would never cease.

Lydia took several pictures that now poignantly remind us of that day. I will never forget the look of anguish and despair on David's face as he watched the shadow of the man his brother once was and held him as he fell asleep in his arms. The next day David and Adam returned for a visit. Alan was walking in the hall with his caregiver, André, and walked right by them, never acknowledging their presence. Naturally they were devastated and returned home upset and sad.

"DAVID AND ALAN, JUNE 2012"

The more I visited, the more I got to know the staff and what an amazing job they were doing. They were respectful of Alan, even when he did not know what he was doing. He would sometimes hit out, but he would then stroke his victim's arm in apology and say "Aaah." They genuinely seemed to care about him. They never seemed to worry about how his behavior affected them, just about doing what was right for Alan and the other patients. The staffing schedule was very consistent. Three shifts a day during the week, always the same people. Then at the weekends, a different group, but again, always the same people: André, Andrus, Topp, Mary, and Annie to name just a few.

They really got to know Alan: his likes and dislikes, his history, and family. They were interested in learning all about him, including his history on the QE2, his football coaching, and his wonderful family. They would ask questions about what they had seen in his books, which they often looked at with and without him. Jeanetta, the manager, was wonderful. Nothing was ever too much trouble, and she took a great interest in all the patients. Their dedication and compassion was really something to behold. They asked for special shampoo to help clear Alan's dry scalp, showered and toileted him regularly, and took all his peculiar behaviors in their stride. There was nothing they would not do for him or me. They took him outside because they knew he liked to pace the circuit out there, and they made sure to go out in the evening when it was cooler or that Alan wore a hat to protect his head from the scorching Arizona sun. They would sit patiently and feed him, even if that meant following him down the hall and feeding him "on the run." Alan was on pureed food as his swallowing had become very poor by that time. They knew he liked cookies and cake and would find a way to get him his sweet puddings, etc.

He was still continent at that time, and he knew when he needed to urinate or have a bowel movement. Alan would do what the staff called "the pee-pee dance." But what happened then was that we would take Alan to the bathroom, and he would stand there and look at us as if to say "Okay, we're here. Now what?" He had no idea what he needed to do and did not associate the toilet with the need or urge to pee. He would eventually be incontinent but only because he no longer knew what to do. He would growl and clench his fists, and it was wise to get out of the confined space as soon as possible. After a while Alan would get frustrated and push the caregiver or me out of the way and try to leave the bathroom, as he had no clue why we were all just standing there. He would not even pull up his shorts before trying to leave. It was quite comical in its own way, and we would laugh, not at him, but at the situation.

It seems strange to say it, but I was never afraid of him then, even when he got so angry and aggressive. I would just pull up his shorts and help him out of the bathroom, and we would continue our walk (well, more pacing really). The only anger he showed was clearly frustration at not understanding what was happening and feeling the urge to urinate but not being able to relieve himself. The staff never took it personally. They would calmly carry on speaking quietly and allowing him to do whatever he wanted.

They had the same philosophy as I did: everything was allowed so long as it did not harm Alan or any of the other residents or staff. I began to feel much more comfortable with Alan's care, and I was becoming used to my new routine. I would visit in the afternoons on my way home from work. We would sit and hold hands or pace the unit together. By then Alan was shuffling badly and unable to change direction if he walked right towards an obstacle. Occasionally we would even do a dance of sorts when he heard music coming from someone's room.

He would bend down to pick up imagined objects from the floor. We would steer him around chairs, residents, carts, anything in his way, as he would walk right into things and try to keep moving. A little like a windup toy that falls off the edge of the table if you don't turn it around. His "off" switch was definitely completely broken, and Alan would rarely stop for rest without direction. He would just keep walking up and down the unit, around the lounge area, round the pool table, and back up the hallway to the other end. He would respond in gibberish to nonexistent conversations with nonexistent people. He would exhaust himself and then sleep for long periods in between.

On June 26 Alan had an appointment with Dr. Y at the Alzheimer's Institute. The staff arranged everything: a caregiver to accompany him, transport, and copies of his latest records. I met Alan and Rhonda, one of his caregivers, at the hospital. He had been showered, freshly shaved, and was wearing clean clothes and shoes, ready for the appointment.

Dr. Y. appeared quite shocked at Alan's deterioration. It had been about eight months since he had last seen him. Alan had been given a little medication to keep him calm during the journey, and he spent the entire appointment dozing in the wheelchair. Dr. Y. seemed quite upset and did not really know what to say, as he knew, as did I, Alan was close to the end of his journey through FTD and Alzheimer's disease. He read the doctor's notes from Maravilla with interest and made some slight changes to medications. Alan's ability to swallow was almost nonexistent. Dr. Y. and I were both in agreement that the time had come to put Alan's end-of-life wishes into effect. He would not be resuscitated should a cardiac or respiratory emergency occur.

And so it was written in his chart that he was a DNR. Do not resuscitate.

That had been his wish in 2009, and in fact, throughout his life whenever the discussion would arise. I would, of course, honor that wish. Dr. Y. suggested it was time to get hospice services involved, so we could make Alan's remaining time as comfortable as possible.

I knew the day was coming, but I wanted to scream, "Not yet, not yet!"

Despite all our preparations and the slow progress of Alan's disease, it seemed the end was hurtling towards us at great speed like a runaway train with no way of stopping it.

The end of the track was in sight.

"LAST KISSES, JULY 2012"

"ALAN, 4TH JULY, 2012"

Twenty-Four

HOSPICE

On June 27, 2012, with the help of Jeanetta, our family enlisted the involvement of Hospice of the Valley and they sent an RN liaison to do their assessment. They would provide a nurse and a nursing assistant several times a week to review Alan's condition and help the Maravilla staff with his personal care. They also provided a social worker to help Adam and me through the upcoming difficult times.

Rhonda, the social worker, was wonderful. She was extremely supportive, even offering to bring Alan a milkshake from McDonald's once she knew he liked them. She listened to Adam and me. She even came to my house to talk with us. Adam had a terrible time during that period, developing all kinds of physical symptoms that were manifestations of his inner pain and anguish. During the conversations with Rhonda, he was honest and brave. I know it was difficult for him to discuss his feelings with a relative stranger, but he knew he could not keep it inside.

Alan even allowed the new staff to help him with bathing. He was unaware of his incontinence and other needs. He had become totally dependent, although still able to walk the hall. He appeared to have developed severe stiffness in his joints and found it difficult to stand from the chair or get up from his bed without assistance. He had lost sixty-five pounds by then, and he was frail and weak, although the staff reported that he continued to lash out unpredictably when startled or frustrated. There was no strength in his swatting, of course, and he was not threatening in any way anymore. Alan was still able to take very small amounts of yoghurt-consistency food with medications crushed and mixed in. However, afterwards he would cough to try to clear his throat, and we could hear gurgling in his chest and throat. That meant that he was aspirating, inhaling food and liquid into his lungs, instead of swallowing it down his esophagus into his stomach. He would "pocket" his food in his cheeks, rather like a hamster, as he would forget to swallow and the reflex became more sporadic.

He was sleeping more and more and walking less and less, becoming easily fatigued at the slightest effort as he became more undernourished.

Around that time, because of the swallowing difficulties, Alan developed aspiration pneumonia. The liquid and food going down into his lungs had caused an infection. The doctor ordered antibiotics, to which I initially agreed, but when I thought about it later that evening, I decided after that episode, we would no longer give Alan anything that would prolong his agony and despair. It was not what he wanted, and it was painful for everyone in our family to see.

Comfort care was the name of the game.

Alan still seemed to recognize me at that point. He would return my kisses, but it did occur to me he might return kisses to anyone. If I put my face close to his and smiled, it appeared that he recognized a face, but perhaps not to whom the face actually belonged. Maybe just a vague someone he knew. Who knows? Maybe that was just my fancy and an attempt to reassure myself that he knew I was still there and doing my best for him.

The decline in Alan's condition continued over the next few weeks. There was less movement, more fatigue, and more sleeping. It was usual for him to be sleeping when I visited. Even if he woke, he would soon drift back to sleep again. The staff informed me he was taking very little food and refusing drinks. I would stop by on my way home from work. Many times I would just sit and hold his hand, watching him sleep. He seemed so peaceful, not in any discomfort at all. He was so infant-like then. Alan would sometimes awaken and look up at me sitting at his bedside. He would give me a little smile and then turn over and go back to sleep.

My heart and soul were assassinated every time. I would sit with tears rolling down my face. I understand how people would offer to give up their own lives to save that of someone they love. I would have done it in a heartbeat.

During that time I began to collect pictures and videos of Alan's life and the wonderful times we had shared together and as a family. It was very therapeutic reminiscing about those times, and I found it very comforting. I made a tribute video, contacted a mortuary, and put together an order of service for Alan's memorial celebration. Alan had said all our lives whenever the subject came up that he did not want to be buried.

"Don't ever put me in a box in a hole in the ground," he would say. It was somewhat of a paradox, this fear of being in the dark alone, for a man who also always said, "When you're dead, you're dead."

So cremation it was then. The pragmatist in me raised her head and used those tasks to get through some very dark days indeed.

On Sunday, September 9, Alan was sleeping again when I arrived. The staff reported he had been up walking in the morning with them, but he not eaten anything that day or the previous day. The walking continued out of habit. He was losing strength quickly, and I knew he could not keep up the fight for too much longer. He was sleeping so much that he could not take anything in, including fluids. I knew it was truly the beginning of the end. No one can survive more than a few days without fluids, as we all know.

On Monday, September 10, the downslide continued. In the medical field, we call it "circling the drain." Not a very nice phrase, I know, but we often use humor to get through difficult situations. I visited after work. I was moving slowly myself then, as I dreaded seeing my once-healthy, muscled, tanned, and fit husband looking thin, wasted, and oblivious to everything around him. I was pulled in two opposing directions: reluctant to visit and scared to miss one single minute.

The next day I left work early and went straight to Maravilla. Alan was sleeping again, completely unaware that I was there. On my way home, the hospice nurse, who had arrived just after I left, called me and said that as Alan could no longer take fluids, it would probably only be a matter of days before he could no longer go on.

I knew that of course, having seen the same situation many times through-out my career. I knew it, but I could not admit it to myself. I was just waiting for someone to tell me and confirm my worst fears. I called Adam and told him I was on my way to his house. I was unable to say anymore as I was crying so much. When I arrived at Adam's home, he told me he was convinced I had come to tell him his dad was gone.

I said, "As if I would do that, not call you to come to the care center but come to your house to tell you!"

We laughed a little, and he said he had not really thought it through. We called Chris and David, and they arranged to get to Alan as soon as possible. Chris arrived the following afternoon, Wednesday, September 12. Amanda was, by that time, heavily pregnant with their third son, and so she was unable to come with him. He told me he was not sure if he could face seeing his dad but knew he needed to, as it might be his last chance. I am sure the agony of his daughter's death the year before was resurrected by the pain he was feeling for his dad. We went together. Alan was very sleepy, but thankfully there was a brief flash of recognition. I was so happy Chris had that to keep in his memory.

The next day, Adam, Chris, and I visited together. I had called in to work on Tuesday, and I told them I would not be back for the foreseeable future, as I had no idea what the next few days would bring. When we arrived Alan was in bed once again, too weak to get up. He did try to sit up and was obviously aware of our presence and voices. He reached out a shaky arm towards us as a single tear slid slowly down his left cheek. Chris took that as a sign his dad truly knew that we were there and that he loved us.

I choose not to doubt that.

I slept in Alan's room that night, in the chair at the side of his bed. His room-mate was noisy, snoring, farting, tossing and turning all night. There was a thin curtain dividing us, but I could not sleep anyway. Alan was restless and anxious. I was so afraid to leave him, even though there was nothing I could do but be there for him, as I had promised I would when we took our vows.

"In sickness and in health, till death us do part."

The last phrase and the last phase were here.

What? Already? Surely not.

Twenty-Five

FINAL DAYS

David arrived on Friday, September 14. He took the long five-hour drive from Los Angeles straight to Maravilla and met me there. My heart broke as I watched the man I had known since he was ten years old look at his big brother lying there while he was unable to help him. He was very shocked at Alan's appearance, even though it had only been a few weeks since he saw him last. David sat with Alan for hours just looking at him, touching him occasionally, and talking softly to him.

Adam and Chris came over later that day and we sat together, sometimes quietly, often loudly. Sometimes we talked to each other, sometimes to Alan. We included him as if he would respond. We sat together and talked as we always had: funny, irreverent, and downright loud. The noise of our family's love for all things ironic, sarcastic, and rude could be heard down the hall. We laughed about the same silly stuff that all families have in them. Those things that seem ridiculous to other people but make us laugh because of our family ties.

We cried too about the times we would have without him. The trips we would never take. The birthdays and anniversaries we would celebrate without him. The dinners and holidays we would never spend together. We cried silently, noisily, alone, and together.

By then Alan had copious secretions collecting in his throat. He was unable to swallow his saliva at all, and he was coughing almost continuously.

We got him up and sat him in a high-back chair for a while. That did seem to help a little. He was very anxious, panicking like a drowning man, which, in effect he was, as he was unable to breathe or understand what was happening. He was prescribed morphine and Ativan, which helped to calm him down a lot.

David was amazing. In all the years I have known him, I have never seen such a tender, caring side of him. He helped the aides to get Alan up, back in bed, turned him, touched his face tenderly, and spoke softly when Alan was agitated.

That night Alan was started on another drug called Robinul, which helped to dry up the secretions and relieved his anxiety and the feeling of drowning. His nurse that night, Andrew, was very caring and kind. He came to the room religiously every two hours with the medication, which eventually calmed Alan down. He put it under his tongue. There were no painful shots, and Alan didn't have to swallow it. The gurgling and coughing noises and restlessness were very distressing for all of us.

Eventually I went home to catch a few hours of sleep. I didn't get much sleep, if any at all. I don't really remember. I showered, changed, and went back.

The next day when I returned the staff had kindly moved Alan's roommate to another room and made up the bed, so I could lie down and stay the night. Alan was still restless, although a little less so than the day before. The coughing continued, but it was decreasing as Alan became calmer and more somnolent. He would have periods, however, of extreme agitation when he would arch his back off the bed and kick his legs downwards. I am sure he was stiff and uncomfortable. We kept up the regime of sedation and pain medication, turning him every two hours like clockwork. As the day went by Alan slipped further and further into a serene and peaceful calm.

I ran an application on my Kindle that played soothing ocean noises: lapping waves, and seagulls in the distance. I hoped they would bring him some sense of comfort and tranquility. Perhaps evoke some sense of the oceans he loved so much.

Typical of our family, we found humor even in our darkest hours. Three or four times a day the staff would take some of the residents outside in the yard to smoke. They would shuffle, stagger, totter, whatever it took to get outside for their fix. Some were wheeled in wheelchairs by the staff. It was a small pleasure the staff could give to those people who had so little joy left in their lives.

The reason it became funny was because David, to take a break from bedside-sitting, joined the "Maravilla Smokers Club." David doesn't smoke, but he would go outside and join them, enjoying their uninhibited outbursts or their silence, depending on their condition. When he came back he would tell us funny little stories about things they had said and done. It lightened the mood for everyone. We shared the stories with Alan too, because we knew he would find them funny. The old lady, Mary, who resided across the hall from Alan's room would shout out completely unrestrainedly. The smiles generated by some of the conversations and interactions that took place at our end of the hall by the exit door were a welcome relief.

I sent David, Adam, and Chris home for some rest, food, and showers. They needed the break. I wanted some time alone with my love too. Time to sit with him, to talk to him, and to lie with him. I lay next to him on his narrow hospital bed, my head on his chest, quietly talking about things we had done, places we had seen, things we had laughed about. I cried, I laughed, and I ribbed him about his irritating little habits.

I whispered, "Do you remember that time when…"

I talked and talked about our whole life.

Our whole thirty-eight years summarized in one night.

Bizarre.

But mostly, I just lay next to him, holding his hand, kissing his cheeks, his lips, his forehead, his hands, and his eyes. My own face was wet with tears as we listened to the sound of the Kindle waves crashing onto the rocks on an imaginary beach far, far away. Knowing that we would never share our dream place to live, by the beach.

Throughout Alan's illness I had always guarded his privacy very carefully. I knew he would only want to see people who genuinely cared for him, not those just coming out of a warped sense of curiosity or duty. Some of the people who cared for both of us just could not face the pain of seeing him that way. On Saturday September 15, I invited our friends Bob and Carole Glass over to visit Alan for one last time. They were the only people I asked. I knew how much it would mean to them and also to Alan if he could know. They sat quietly at the bedside. Bob held Alan's hand and said very little. He was shocked it had come to that. I know they appreciated they were able to say their last goodbyes.

After they left the night went by slowly. I slept intermittently, waking to every little change in Alan's breathing or movement. The staff was the epitome of caring: they were kind and respectful. They came in punctually every two hours with medication and offers to reposition Alan. They never compromised Alan's dignity or showed any sign we were a nuisance to them.

Sunday, September 16, was the longest day of my life.

The room was pretty crowded. David, Adam and his wife Pamela, Chris, and I spent the whole day sitting in the room, either together or in twos and threes. Sometimes each of us was alone with Alan to say our last words and to share our love with him for the last time. We thought it would be Alan's last day, and we meant to spend as much of it as possible with him.

When we were alone, I lay on the bed next to Alan again, stroking his forehead or arm and talking to him about how thankful I was for the life we had shared. I told him over and over that I loved him and that I knew he loved me.

David had said the day before he did not want to be there at the end. I respected and understood his wishes.

Alan's breathing became more regular that day, and he seemed a little more at peace as the levels of medications reached a point where they were working for him as they were supposed to. His heart was beating strongly, however. It seemed as though he could stay in that suspended state forever, between worlds, but comfortable and no longer in any distress.

I was reminded of the time when Adam was lying in the ICU after his accident and how painful that was for Alan. He'd had to leave the room frequently.

How I missed him then. I wanted to have him stand there with me in that surreal situation and hold my hand as we did when Adam was hurt. The scene was reversed as Adam stood and watched over his dad. It was an eerie twist on a horrible memory.

At 12:30 a.m., David left saying, "I know he'll still be here in the morning, so I'm going home for some sleep. I'll be back tomorrow."

I'm not sure if he was secretly hoping he would not be there when Alan died and that was why he left. Adam and Pamela were persuaded to leave at around 1:30 a.m., as Adam was asleep in the chair anyway. I promised to call if there was any change. Chris would not leave us, and he lay on the extra bed as I sat in the chair at Alan's bedside. Eventually he fell asleep too, leaving my darling and me alone.

Side-by-side as always.

Through really good times and less-than-good times, we had stood together, always together; sometimes at odds but never divided. Throughout the night Alan's steady, regular breathing pattern continued. Sometime around 3:00 a.m. I had to stand, as I was stiff and aching. I was tired of sitting, lying, and standing. I went outside to get some air.

It was a beautiful, warm Arizona night. The sky was clear, and I looked up at those same stars we had looked at together so many times from the sun beds by our pool. Alan would never see those stars again. I shouted out loud to the endless night sky, "Please make it stop now. We can't take any more!"

I sobbed and bawled, begging for our ordeal to be over. I was ready.

I went back inside and sat by Alan's bed. I held his hand and begged him to give up his fight. I told him it was okay to let go and to stop fighting. He had been a fighter all his life, one way or another, and he never knew when to give up. I gave him permission to be free of the horrible disease that had destroyed our lives, even though every part of me wanted to hold him forever and never let him go. There was a terrible feeling of being pulled from two sides in a freakish tug-of-war.

One of the final scenes at the end of one of my favorite movies, *E.T.*, came to mind:

Elliot: "Stay."

E.T.: "Come."

We had all said our goodbyes during our private moments over the last few days and enough was enough.

The longest night of my life was also the most painful one.

The staff came in regularly throughout the night, always respectful of our privacy and attending to Alan's and my needs. They asked if we wanted them to turn Alan, but he was so comfortable, we let him be.

Pressure sores were no longer an issue for him.

Twenty-Six

THE MUSIC'S STOPPED, IT'S TIME TO GO HOME

*M*onday, September 17, 2012, was our son Chris's twenty-ninth birthday.

Chris and I lay still. Chris was dozing, but I was unable to sleep. We lay quietly next to one another on the tiny hospital bed, huddled close together. Just as we had been that first day of his life in 1983 with his dad sleeping close by.

I listened to Alan's slow but regular breathing pattern in anguish.

Amanda called at 4:00 a.m., so she could be the first to wish Chris happy birthday. She was unable to sleep and felt sad and detached from what was happening.

At 6:00 a.m. the staff brought in breakfast for us. Alan's breathing was beginning to slow even more.

Around 8.30 a.m. David returned, saying, "I told you he would still be here today."

Chris left at about 9:00 a.m. to shower, and I said I would go and do the same when he returned, although I didn't really intend to leave at all. David and I sat on either side of Alan at the head of the bed. David to Alan's left, and I was to his right. We held his hands and talked to him as he slowly slipped away. His breathing became more shallow but still regular. His heart beat was regular, although less strong. We watched his carotid pulse continue to beat strongly in his neck as the end came slowly, slowly.

Susan called at 10:05 a.m. David held the phone to Alan's ear, and Susan spoke gently and lovingly to her brother, telling Alan she loved him, and it was okay to go now.

David and I watched as the breaths became slower and slower, shallower and fainter. The pulse in Alan's neck grew weaker and weaker as the minutes ticked by.

Eventually, a breath came and went. It was the last one. There were no more to follow. The color, such as was remaining, drained from Alan's face, and the pulse in his neck disappeared. I asked David to note the time: 10:22 a.m. Adam and Pamela walked in at 10:24 a.m. We hugged and kissed as we sobbed with relief, sadness, and grief.

Adam said his dad was whole and free again, the vibrant, loving man we had known. He could speak, walk, and function and be the man he was before the vehemently horrible disease struck all our lives.

I hoped so.

I am a nurse. I have seen many people pass in and out of this life. I've seen births, deaths, and everything in between.

I have confirmed absence of respirations, pulse, and response in many, many people. I have certified deaths and told families who arrived too late that their loved one had waited until they left to depart this life.

I have stood and cried with the newly shocked.

I have sat and held the hands of those who would have otherwise died alone. Strangers drawn together by sad situations.

Just life rolling inexorably on.

Being in that situation with someone who is part of your very being, your soul, your spirit, and your world, is surreal to say the least.

The Maravilla staff seemed genuinely upset at Alan's death. During those last few days and hours, staff members came from all over the facility to say their goodbyes to him. One girl said she had only taken care of him once but wanted to come and pay her respects.

We were so touched.

The end brought a weird kind of comfort. We had all suffered along with Alan every step of the way. The pain, anger, disbelief, and exhaustion were finally over. We could only hope Alan's pain and frustration were over too. Over those last few days, I had felt cheated. In other terminal diseases such as cancer, the victim is often cognizant right up until close to the end. That means they too get to say their goodbyes and utter their last words of love.

My last kisses were completely one-sided. Alan was unaware of his last kiss and the love we showered upon him. Unaware of his insidious descent into whatever comes next.

Being in the throes of death with an already altered mind is just not fair.

I walked away from my darling reluctantly, supported on either side by our wonderful sons.

I did not want to leave him there.

David and Pamela were waiting outside as the boys and I said our final goodbyes. That walk through the door of Maravilla for the last time—I cannot really describe it.

It is so hard to fathom you will never see a person again. I cannot imagine what leaving their baby daughter, Madison, behind must have been like for Chris and Amanda.

I only know when you hear old clichés like, "A piece of my heart has been torn out," it does not even begin to describe the physical pain caused by leaving your husband's mortal remains behind somewhere, even though you know his spirit or soul or whatever you believe in, is no longer present.

All rationality leaves you. You know the person is dead. You know he will not be coming back. But some strange power overtakes your rationale and replaces it with totally irrational thoughts. Ideas like: "How do I know he is really gone? What if there has been a mistake?"

Even reading this now, I can still feel the panic and the urge to run back into Maravilla and stop them from taking Alan away from me.

Before we left for the last time, Chris asked the nurse if she would be sure that when Alan was picked up by the mortuary people, he was wearing his favorite Manchester United team shirt and shorts Chris had brought along. It was his last gift to his dad. Later that week when Adam, Chris, David, and I visited the funeral home to make the final arrangements, I asked the funeral director what Alan was wearing when they picked him up from Maravilla before they sent him to the crematorium. He replied, "A Manchester United shirt and shorts."

Maravilla magic again.

⌢⌐

The next day, Tuesday, September 18, Chris began making calls to various friends and family all over the world. We sat on my patio in the morning sun and got out my old address book to begin the process of sharing the horrible news.

As I opened the book, a small folded purple piece of paper floated out. It said: "Have a terrific Tuesday!" When I opened it, inside it said: "Love You xxxx." And there was a large lipstick kiss.

I thought I had got rid of all my little daily notes when I moved out of our house, but that one was still there. It made Chris and me smile.

I like to believe it was Alan's last little wave goodbye. A fanciful idea, but it helped a lot.

There were several other little coincidences similar to the love note that happened during that first couple of weeks. First, I received a call from a man called John, who had been referred to me by the funeral home in reference to officiating at Alan's memorial service. He said I had an unusual name, and he had married a couple with a similar name earlier in the year and wondered if we were related.

He was the man who had performed the wedding ceremony for Adam and Pamela in January.

The second thing was that after the call from John, our friend Steve Wooster inadvertently forwarded a reply to one of his business emails to me. The recipient had the same last name as the officiant John.

In the days and weeks that followed, we talked, planned, and reminisced, but we were generally numb. Unbearably sad but accepting. Chris and I continued to plan for the service. He was wonderful. He took the whole thing out of my hands and just got on with it. Chris got the orders of service printed, made calls, edited the video, and went to the funeral home to check out the equipment. I think it was his way of dealing with it, keeping busy and feeling productive.

I am sure the situation brought back black memories of his daughter's death just a short time before, but he really stepped up and took the lead. I was so proud of him.

Adam, I think, felt like I did: sad, relieved, and astounded at how quickly the "slow progression" had finally gone. We were both still a little angry at the injustice of it all. Both of us were immobilized by the pain and grief.

Pamela was wonderful during that time. She cooked and cleaned at my house, making sure everyone was comfortable and well fed. She did whatever needed to be done. She volunteered her own services and those of her mother, Alma, to cater the memorial service lunch. Pamela, Chris, and Lydia pulled the whole thing together, allowing Adam, David, and I to get on with our grieving. Relinquishing control was a relatively new experience for me.

Lydia, too, was especially strong. I think out of everyone, she could really relate to how I was feeling as she and David have a very similar relationship to Alan and I. Alan and David were alike in so many ways. Lydia is kind, patient, tolerant, loving, and amazingly selfless.

During the next few weeks people were so kind, sending food, flowers, fruit, cards, and messages. It was truly heartwarming to receive the outpouring of support.

The memorial service was on September 27. We had arranged it so far out from the day Alan died to allow time for anyone who wanted to come from England to make arrangements. As it turned out, it was not possible for that to happen.

I wrote in my journal: "This is the last thing I can do for him. I will do my best to hold it together today and do it well for him. I feel the strength of my dad and Madison, Beryl and Alan urging me to have courage…"

When I arrived at the mortuary with Adam and Chris I really did not think I could go through with it. I said so aloud to Lydia as I entered the chapel.

Seeing all of his pictures and favorite things gathered there in that place and the urn with his ashes was like the end of a movie you were really enjoying that had a surprise ending. Or a book you loved and didn't ever want to finish reading.

I wanted to turn and run. I had imagined it, planned it, but I never actually thought it would be real. In the end, it turned out to be a comforting experience. Many people came. Those who offered or were asked to speak were amazing, including Tony Shepherd, Bob Glass, and John Marlor. There were even a couple of surprise speakers: Nedim, a good friend from Palm Desert and one of Adam's friends, Ted.

Alan's cousin, Tony, who lives in New York, flew in the night before the service. He and Alan had always been close growing up, and they had worked together for quite a while when we had the Three Shires Wine Bar while Tony was in college.

Tony's eulogy was wonderful. He had everyone laughing at some of the antics and escapades the two of them had got up to in their younger days, some of which I didn't even know about!

The service and lunch afterwards were not somber affairs. There were some tears of course, but also a great deal of laughter and reminiscing. When we got home the boys all went out to our local bar, Alan's favorite watering hole, Crackerjacks, for drinks. Around thirty people turned out to say "cheers" to Alan. David, Adam, and Chris were so touched by that. It was affirmation that their dad and brother was a great guy and that other people knew that too.

On October 4 I flew to Los Angeles to remember Alan at a beautiful gathering of our friends who live there. David and Lydia opened their home and made a sad occasion into something lovely and touching. It was a wonderful day with many tears, much laughter, and a lot of love. The guest book was signed by all, and we watched the tribute video of Alan and our family. Everyone had a special memory about a time they had spent with Alan and were stunned by what had happened.

Then, on October 14, our friends and family in England held a memorial service for Alan on a Sunday afternoon in my hometown of Marple. Our friend Danny closed his pub for the occasion, and Alan Harvey provided food and drink for about fifty people, including Susan and Lorraine, their families, and my mother. They were all people we grew up with and spent lots of time with before we emigrated in 1999. They showed the video I had put together, and everyone signed the guest book that had been at the Phoenix memorial and at David and Lydia's house the week before.

I am a nurse. When Alan was sick, I knew what to do.

I no longer knew what to do. I didn't know where to begin being "Debbie" and not "Alan and Debbie" anymore, even though we had not really been Alan and Debbie for quite some time.

Now I had to dance solo and look at the stars alone.

"Stars"

I lit a fire with the love you left behind
And it burned wild and crept up the mountain side
I followed your ashes into outer space
I can't look out the window, I can't look at this place.
I can't look at the stars
They make me wonder where you are
Stars, up on heaven's boulevard
And if I know you at all, I know you've gone too far
So I, I can't look at the stars.
All those times we looked up at the sky
Looking out so far, it felt like we could fly

And now I'm all alone in the dark of night
And the moon is shining, but I can't see the light.
And I can't look at the stars
They make me wonder where you are
Stars, up on heaven's boulevard
And if I know you at all, I know you've gone too far
So I, I can't look at the stars.

Stars, Stars, they make me wonder where you are
Stars, up on heaven's boulevard
And if I know you at all, I know you've gone too far
So I can't look at the stars.

—Grace Potter
(permission for use requested)

........I really, really can't.

AFTER

Twenty-Seven

THE MUSIC PLAYS ON, BUT THE DANCERS HAVE LEFT THE FLOOR

*A*lan will always be part of my children, my grandchildren, and me. Without him there would be no us.

After means after we grew strong and brave.

After we learned to keep moving.

After our family love is stronger and deeper.

After we feel a little less safe and a little less confident.

After Maravilla.

After is now.

But also, after, we are wiser, braver, and kinder because of who Alan was, is, and always will be to us.

On October 9, 2012, I wrote: "You know that feeling when you leave somewhere or go somewhere, and you feel like you left something behind? That's how I feel ALL THE TIME!"

That's because I did. I left him behind at Maravilla Care Center. I wish I could get those memories out of my head and focus on the ones from 1974, or 1983, or 1985, or 2002. I look back at the videos from our Pacific Highway road trip in 2006 and smile. I had almost forgotten what Alan's voice sounded like.

160

Any memories, even those from less-than-good times, are better than some of the ones I have. It's hard to get them out of my head. It's not that I'm living in the past or want to. It's that I want to have *our* future and not the one I am being forced to live. It feels like someone else's.

Oh, I make plans and talk big about the trips I take and plan to take.

I experience stolen moments from my comfortable grief.

I wear nice clothes and try to look good. I exercise, eat well, and generally take care of myself. I get compliments from people about how well I look and that I seem to be doing. And I am. I am doing well.

Whatever that means. If doing well means you appear not to be a quivering wreck who breaks down and cries at every opportunity, then yes, I am doing well. I remain irreparably damaged by the cruel loss. Our love cannot be replicated or replaced or got "over." You don't get over it.

Everyone wants you to be doing well because that feels more comfortable for them. They try to set you up with their friends, because they think you might be lonely and need some company. This is just because it makes them feel better that you won't be alone.

Alone is okay. I can time travel, cry, relax, dance, sing—whatever I like. But I like to do it alone, because then I don't have to explain it to anyone.

I can't tell you how to be a widow or a widower. I can't tell you how to handle your grief and pain. I don't think anyone really gets it. Even other people who have been through similar experiences can't understand your experience, nor you theirs. It's just too personal and unique. At first I read books about grief and widowhood, but none of them sounded like me. The first time I talked about "my late husband" I shocked myself. Then I smiled a little at the irony. He would hate to be described as "late." Alan Thelwell was never late for anything in his life.

From 1974 until 2010 my life with Alan was at various times funny, irritating, painful, fun, argumentative, tough, tearful, happy, and joyous. But it was always full of love.

From 2010 until September 17, 2012, it was infuriating, sad, baffling, funny, tough, and downright scary but always full of love.

That's because nothing can destroy the love, however hard it tries. Not pain, not sorrow, not some bastard disease. The bastard disease just makes you love more in an attempt to beat it, even when you know that such fighting is futile. The human spirit is a formidable thing indeed.

Rose Kennedy said: "It has been said, 'time heals all wounds.' I do not agree. The wounds remain. In time, the mind, protecting its sanity, covers them with scar tissue and the pain lessens. But it is never gone."

I agree with Rose. I may never tire of the pain. That probably sounds strange. It is oddly comforting, like a direct connection to Alan. Because, for the last year of his life, pain was one of the strongest feelings I had, next to love. The love never waned, and it still hasn't. Even in the darkest hours, it was still him and me, just like since we first met. He felt it too, I know. It was so usual, so normal, and so ingrained that no bastard of a disease could deprive us of it.

There were so many questions and so much emotion. What felt like the end was only the beginning.

Now it is about me having to face my own feelings, fears, and thoughts. I had been able to sideline most of that before by dealing with practicalities and the needs of others. Now there is no hiding place.

I am the subject of scrutiny:

"How are you doing?" "How are you?" "Give me a call." "Let's go out for dinner/movies." "Why don't you come over?"

I know was all meant kindly, but it was just too much.

I was floating in a comfortable cocoon for a while. Smiling outwardly like some ridiculous Cheshire Cat. My home became my haven. I was safe there, and I could shut out the horror from my little bubble. After I returned to work I took to only going to places where the people there didn't know me or know what had happened in my life: the gym, a new Zumba class, stores, and other places where I could be anonymous. Being with people who knew me and my history was sometimes just too much.

I met a woman at my Zumba class who had also lost her husband to FTD two years before. There were so many similarities in our lives that it was uncanny. I am a little ashamed to say I am not a good friend. I don't often pursue relationships with people outside the inner circle of my immediate family, Adam, Chris, and their families, David and Lydia, and a few close friends.

I don't feel the need.

I don't think I will ever recover completely from the experience of losing Alan. There is too much history, too much time, and too much love that can never be surpassed. Why would I try? It would be disloyal and unfaithful—not right. There is physical pain too, deep, deep inside. I feel like the love we felt for one another was like nothing anyone else knows. It was a special secret known only to us. Oh, I know everyone who loves deeply feels the same way, but it never leaves you. Utter sadness prevailed then and still does. I could not, and still cannot, fathom how that much pain could ever go away. I was afraid if it did, my memories would disappear too, and I could not let that happen, nor did I want to. I still don't.

I don't think sadness is a bad thing. It can be a pleasant kind of feeling. Does that make me clinically depressed? I'm not sure. I don't really care if it does. I am a good person with ideals and values. I don't hurt anyone. I have a job in which I help people to help other people. I live a healthy life, and I know how to have fun and laugh along with other people. I see the humor in everyday life. I see the humor and irony in what happened to Alan, our family, and me.

Oh yes, there was humor almost every day at some point. The old saying "You have to laugh or you'd cry" was definitely true for us. We would laugh while we were crying. We would laugh so much it made us cry. The human spirit can endure so much. The endurance builds strength, like exercise for your psyche.

It is hard to forget what Alan looked like at the end of his life. Old, sick, scared, and thin—then suddenly, gone. He did not look like my strong, funny, loving, passionate, loyal, proud, and often infuriating Alan.

There are so many questions left unanswered. Did Alan know, in the turmoil of his dementia, the love we felt for him? Did he know we were there with him? Laughing and crying with him and for him? I can only hope so, but after, in the here and now, it doesn't really matter. I could write intense, spiritual things about how I feel he is still with me, or he's looking down and smiling at us with Madison at his side. I could but I can't.

Alan was never a believer in spiritual things (unless constantly watching re-runs of *The Ghost Whisperer* counts), so why would I think he could be around me now in his afterlife? You catch me in a kind of lie here, by the way, because I talk to him all the time.

I know other people may find such thoughts comforting, but I don't. I make no apology for that. He is gone, not here, absent, deceased, expired—dead. Like the parrot in the sketch from *Monty Python*. That's not as unfeeling as it sounds. Yes, his body is dead. But the angels didn't take him. He didn't rise above his withered, bony body and ascend to a "better place."

What is that about by the way? A better place? My son Chris told me when someone said that to him after Madison died, he said, "No, she isn't in a better place. A better place would be here with me and the rest of her family."

And I agree. A better place for Alan would be here with us, enjoying the things we are finding it hard to enjoy without him. But we would not want him back altered as he was. We want the old Alan back.

The Alan I met at Sergeant Peppers in 1974. The Alan who watched his sons come into the world in 1983 and 1985. The Alan who caught a football kicked out at a Rod Stewart concert. The Alan who drove me mad, because he was a nasty drunk. The Alan who irritated the crap out of me when he was being stubborn and unreasonable even before the FTD. The Alan that held my hand when I was sick, pissed off at work, or needed defending against some insult to my beauty, ability, or actions, which he always considered perfect (Bless him!). The Alan I love.

If there is an "after" for Alan, I really hope there is someone or something that will keep an eye on him, as he will definitely need supervision, especially if they have beer or gin, champagne or marijuana. Romantic notions of a serene, tranquil afterlife somehow don't fit with Alan.

I do know he would appreciate the places I have scattered his ashes over the last few months: at the top of South Mountain, out by Apache lake, in the Caribbean (courtesy of Steve), in the Stretford end goal at his beloved Manchester United's stadium, Old Trafford, and into the Pacific Ocean.

Even as I write these words, I cannot believe I am saying them. This is *my* Alan Thelwell we're talking about, right?

Thelly from Blazes?

Chris and Adam's dad? Jack Mason, Zane, Madison, and Cruz's granddad?

Steve, Les, Bob, John, and everyone else's friend?

What?

October 30, 2012, would have been our thirty-sixth wedding anniversary. It was six weeks after he died. The night before was the worst. I was sobbing, questioning, and asking myself "If he is there, why does he not give me a sign?"

I am not a religious person, but I prayed, fervently hoping that wherever he is, he is not wandering, still confused, and looking for me. I tried to reassure myself, that if an afterlife exists, all pain and infirmity is healed there and he now knows what happened.

In the last three months of 2012 our wedding anniversary, my birthday, his birthday, and Christmas came and went. Christmas was always a big deal in our family. Like everyone else, we had our traditions and funny little family quirks. Although Alan had not been living at home the previous year, it was still very strange to have our holiday without him. I flew up to Washington to watch the arrival of our newest grandson, Cruz Alan, on December 8. I was angry Alan would never get to see or hold him. But I can let it go, because my anger is not productive. It won't change anything.

In November I was in San Diego for a business conference, and then Lydia joined me afterwards to celebrate my birthday. On the plane on the way home it occurred to me I really wouldn't care if the plane crashed. Maybe there was a chance I could be with Alan. The only thing that stopped me from continuing along that train of thought was my children. They are grown men, but they will always be my children. I simply would not do that to them.

There were times during the first three months I cried on the way to work, at work behind the closed door of my office, and barely made it out of the door to my car in the afternoon before I broke down in tears. I cried every day. Music, photos, sunsets, the ocean, TV shows, and movies—everything reminded me of Alan

I begged out loud many times for him to come to me, to give me some kind of sign. If he was there, I needed to know. This is common, I know, in newly bereaved people. One night, it occurred to me that if he somehow came back, he wouldn't know where I was. He had never been to the place I now called home. What if he was waiting for me at our old house? I hoped he was not scared and alone. When I read back over my journal entries from a year before, prior to Alan going into the psychiatric hospital, it shattered my heart like shards of glass. He was so very afraid.

Now in 2013 we have lived through a New Year and a Father's Day, Madison's birthday, and the second anniversary of her death.

We (for it will always be we) have a new grandson.

Chris and Amanda have moved back to Arizona from Washington. They have separated now. Their relationship simply could not withstand the grief and torment of losing their daughter. Chris lost his baby daughter and his dad in the space of fifteen months. My heart aches for them both.

This year, on the first anniversary of his dad's death, September 17, we celebrated Chris's thirtieth birthday. I'm not sure what the significance of that is or even if there is any. Conversations with David, Lydia, Chris, and Adam tell me we are all still very raw about what happened. It rips my heart in two. We still cannot believe it.

Even now, at the end of the first year, I miss Alan so terribly there is still great physical pain.

I am an amputee. The very core of my being is missing.

I have a life and everything in it to remember him by. I had thirty-eight years with someone who truly loved and understood me. Many people don't get half of that. But understanding the privilege of this does not help.

Now, one year on, I do not think my life is over without Alan; I just know, reluctantly, my life with Alan is over.

I see my life is different. It is still important to me that I live a life of which Alan would approve and want to share. You can't discount almost forty years and not have it influence the next twenty or thirty. I think I can continue my life by fulfilling the plans, hopes, and dreams we shared. I will just be experiencing them alone.

No matter what I do, Alan will still be gone.

I still dance. I joined a Zumba class. I love it. Can't get enough. It's dancing alone, in a group (what a dichotomy), and that is about as much as I want right now.

I am *Dancing With Tears In My Eyes.* (Thank you, Midge Ure and Ultravox.)

Made in the USA
Lexington, KY
20 April 2016